KINGDOM TOOLS FOR TEACHING

For far too long we have viewed the Kingdom of God as only applicable to a future age or applied it exclusively to the church thereby abandoning all the other arenas of life that shape our culture including one of the most important, education. All my life I have been surrounded by educators. My father was an educator, my wife is a first grade teacher, and I even taught for several years at a Midwestern university. Those whom God has called to bring His Kingdom, His presence, wisdom, and the prophetic revealing of Jesus into the classroom will find *Kingdom Tools for Teaching* gives them new tools in creative and thought provoking ways. I highly recommend this book and applaud all those courageous educators who are serving God in our schools and bringing His Kingdom on earth.

BOB HARTLEY
Hartley Institute, Deeper Waters, Inc.

It has long been the desire of Kingdom-minded teachers to transform classrooms to reflect and project what Holy Spirit is saying and doing. *Kingdom Tools for Teaching* equips educators in all types of schools (public, private, Christian, secular) with time tested methods for bringing the heavenly culture to the academic realm. This book is must read for anyone who longs to bring "the little children to Jesus and hinder them not." The techniques presented in it are amazing – we can't wait to use them at our school.

SANDY WOODS
Principal, Comenius School for Creative Leadership

This book stirred my heart and reminded me why I have dedicated so many years to the profession of teaching. It also stirred up my faith for even more of Holy Spirit's intervention in our school. I am personally so proud of my staff members: Sara, Lindsay, and Tawny for pouring their hearts into this labor of love. They are amazing teachers who carry the Kingdom well. Janine Mason has put together not only a great book for teachers who want more of the Kingdom in their classroom, but she has formatted it in such a way to make it a useful guide for educator's discussion groups and professional development. I highly recommend it to all educators who want to welcome Holy Spirit into their classrooms and lesson planning.

DEBI ARMSTRONG
Academic Vice Principal, Bethel Christian School

There is a great need today for the Kingdom of Jesus to once again impact the kingdom of education. Our young adults and children in all places of education are desperate for hope that is only found in the person of Jesus and embodied by the people of Jesus. In this book you will discover many creative and useful tools and concepts that could foundationally shift the culture of your classroom and school. This book is not only for Christian school teachers but also for the public school educator who is hungry to grow in seeing the kingdom in their classroom as well. Read this book as I did, with and open heart and a willingness to adapt it to your classroom and you will be inspired and empowered in new ways to see the Kingdom show up in ways you didn't expect.

AARON HAYES
Educator and Pastor

The set of tools shared in this book are practical, Spirit-filled and easy to apply to any classroom, no matter the age or subject. I have no doubts a teacher who uses these tools will transform their environment into a Kingdom classroom and be motivated to seek the Holy Spirit for new tools. How I wish I had this book when I was in the classroom!

AMY SHOLDT
K-6 Classroom Teacher for 23 Years

Every teacher needs encouragement as they undertake the privilege and challenge of educating the children and young people in their care. What I love about this book is the way it brings together God's tangible hope with practical tools for real classrooms. As I read this book I felt like I was in the company of a wise friend who understood my very real and daily journey as a teacher and encouraged me to partner with the Holy Spirit to receive the heavenly strategies that God has for me. This is a must read for all teachers who desire to know more of God's transforming presence in their lives and in their classrooms.

CLAIRE MCCOURT
High School History Teacher for 10 Years

Whether you teach in public or private school you will be encouraged and motivated by *Kingdom Tools for Teaching*. It is filled with examples of teachers that have learned to ask God and receive His answers to what they need. By partnering with the Holy Spirit they have seen their own teaching styles shift to match both classroom and individual student needs. The more we partner with God the greater our impact will be on our students. *Kingdom Tools for Teaching* is not as much about the methods used by the authors as it is about showing through example how to partner with God in your classroom by imparting faith, hope, love, and trust in God. I know you will be encouraged and inspired!

DON MAYER
Principal, Bethel Christian School

KINGDOM TOOLS FOR TEACHING

Heavenly strategies for real classrooms

JANINE MASON

LINDSAY BROWN • TAWNY NOVOSAD • SARA RUST

KINGDOM TOOLS FOR TEACHING
Heavenly Strategies For Real Classrooms

Cover Design: Josh Stannard
Interior Design: Jonathan McGraw. jonathanmcgraw.net
Author Photos: Tracey Hedge, firefly2u.com

ISBN-13:978-1514226612
ISBN-10:1514226618

To order more books,
other resources or to share your testimonies
contact janinem@ibethel.org

CONTENTS

FOREWORD

About fifty years ago, a strategic shift happened in our country. Our education system was hijacked by an anti-Christ agenda. The result is a generation of people who do not have a Biblical worldview. Children, young people, and young adults are trained to believe that faith in God is a mythical fantasy for the less educated, ignorant, and feeble-minded among us. Hostility toward religion is tolerated and promoted as an effort to rid our society of bigoted, small-minded people. Christianity may be the only group in America that is "cool" to hate. How did our country give up such a principal part of its establishment? Why would so many be willing to walk away from the infrastructure of our foundations?

I believe it largely originates from the practice and understanding of freedom. For some reason, Christianity could not or would not grow to include living in the freedom that Christ died to give us. It is a strange and common redundancy in religious culture to remain in the past. Somehow, we honestly believe that yesterday is the goal, and we seek to stay there in our comfortable securities. But people were created to be free, and if they can't find it in Christ, then they will aggressively look for it somewhere else.

Showing the world the Father is what the church is called to do. We are to imitate Jesus, and He was perfect in putting His father on display in all aspects of His life. If we think we are here to show the world the church or the Bible, then we are drawn into a constricting cycle that is limited to our understanding instead of the constant, mysterious, and expanding adventure of who the Father is. Bringing Heaven to Earth is a calling, a commissioning, and a conundrum. We live believing that God is at work in our lives and in the lives of those around us, but actualizing the supernatural realities of the Christian life can feel like an elusive search.

Putting God back into the classroom can seem like a lost cause. At this point, "God in the classroom" means trying to get church practices such as prayer, devotions, Bible study, or witnessing back into the classroom. There are now layers of defenses established that will "protect" students from these things. We don't need church in the classroom. We need the Kingdom of God in our society—especially in the classroom. In every place where our next generation is learning about how to lead our society into the future, we need them to know, experience, and learn to practice the Kingdom of God.

What you have in your hands is among the first of its kind. This is a training manual in the Kingdom of Heaven. This is how we change generations to come. If you've been looking for how to create a godly revolution around you in the classroom, then you've found what you've been looking for. I know because I've watched for over a decade as these tools, practices, and paradigms have equipped teachers and their students in the supernatural power of God. When I say this, I don't mean Bible study. This book isn't a way to subversively have devotions or church in the classroom. In these pages you will find a template to show children freedom, love, joy, righteousness, hope & power. In other words, you have a tool to show students the Father—much like Jesus showed the Father to everyone He crossed paths with.

Some people, who I know to be experts in this field, are about to show you how to fulfill a deep longing in that teacher heart of yours. I am excited to see this book finally available. God bless you on this journey to turn a generation back to the King.

Danny Silk

LETTER FROM THE AUTHORS

All of us are on a journey. It is a journey of learning to grow the Kingdom of God in a greater way in our lives. It's a lifelong journey of learning, discovery, and relationships. We never "arrive" or have it all figured out. We simply gain more understanding, and often more questions, as we are on our way. We, the authors of this book, are on this journey right along with you. We certainly don't have all the answers, and we are constantly discovering how much more there is to unveil in our quest to bring His Kingdom to our world. Each of us considers ourselves novices in His ways, which keeps us positioned as humble learners.

This is not a manual. This is the testimony of our breakthroughs and the tools that came from them. It is our heart to share these tools to inspire you to find your own and to adapt what we have done to your own classroom or school. Tools in the Kingdom are seldom one size fits all. They are best used how they are discovered—that is, they need to be used in relationship with the one who inspired them, the Holy Spirit. As you read through these pages you will see snapshots of the authors' personal journeys with the Holy Spirit. These journeys are what make the tools work. The teacher's connection with the Holy Spirit is the power behind the tools. Without that relationship guiding you, the tools on the following pages are nothing more than good teaching ideas, valuable but not life-changing.

It is our prayer that as you read, you will be inspired in your own journey with the Holy Spirit, that you will discover your own tools to a new level, and that the tools you find here will become your own revelation in order to build the Kingdom in your classroom. We pray that you will find the courage to embrace the call to discover more of Him in all that you do. We pray that your journey will be marked by the discovery of a loving Father that delights in you more than you can imagine. And we pray that you will find joy and peace and His presence on that journey as you commit yourself to be content but never satisfied.

INTRODUCTION

The Creator of the universe has His eye on the education system of the world and, in particular, on your classroom. His plans for your classroom are exceedingly good. What He wants to do in and through you is beyond what you could ask or even imagine (Ephesians 3:20). He longs to have His presence expressed in every school across the globe, influencing faculty and students alike. His presence in schools is not illegal. In fact many non-believing administrators are welcoming His presence into their schools because of the benefits it brings. They may not realize the source of the peace, honor, or love that is invading their classrooms, but they like what they see and feel when God is there. Because of the impact that these God-carriers are having, administrators are empowering those who bring His presence to new levels of influence in the educational system. The question is not whether or not God has a plan for bringing change. The question is whether or not you will embrace your part of His plan and be a part of this global adventure. Will you embrace change and bring the Kingdom of God to your classroom to a whole new level?

Change always costs us something. We tend to grow to the point that feels comfortable then level off when the cost of change becomes too high. In doing so, we limit our involvement in God's plan for planet earth. You are called to move from "glory to glory" (2 Corinthians 3:18). This sounds wonderful and, as the verse suggests, glorious. The challenge I have noticed is that the gap between one glory and the next is filled with risk, discomfort, and sometimes apparent failure. It is only as I continue to pursue Him and the process of change that I move into the new level of glory that the Bible promises. I urge you to embrace the call to continue to grow and learn, not just in your professional capacity but also in your ability to bring His Kingdom, the expression of His nature, wherever you are. The cost will be high and sometimes the journey will seem painful, but the benefits to your students and to you far outweigh the cost.

There is a process of learning that you see every day and are well acquainted with. You introduce a new concept to your students, and at first it is totally foreign to them. The new tool or skill is hard for them to wield, and they can feel overwhelmed by the sense of not understanding, particularly if they feel like other students are catching on more quickly than they are. As a teacher, you do all you can to minimize the negative emotions of this period. You provide lots of encouragement to the students and give them tools to make the transition as easy as possible.

Whether you are teaching a first grader to read or a high school senior to write a scientific research paper, the same process plays out. It's a process that students expect to go through over and over as they progress through their academic career. The challenge comes for us, as adults, when we reach a point where learning new things is no longer expected or demanded. Being a part of the educational system demands that you keep up with your continuing education units. Primarily these deal with learning new tools and involve change that occurs in the mind. Being in the educational system does not, however, typically address your learning or growth in other areas such as your faith or internal beliefs. These areas are the ones that will need to change if you are going to increase your ability to see His Kingdom expressed in the classroom and beyond. These areas have a greater cost to bring change to, but they are also the ones that bring tremendous benefit. So what do you need to address as you embrace the challenge? What will you have to face in order to grow your ability to see His Kingdom manifested in a greater way in your environment? Fear, risk, and failure are all a part of what is ahead.

Going on a journey of growth with God can be a scary deal. A natural journey to adventure into uncharted territory means that you never quite know what is around the next corner. A journey with God into new spiritual territory is not so different. You can try to predict what you will need for the journey and to prepare, but you can't be sure where this great adventure will take you. It is always a risk. There is no guarantee that everything will work out just perfectly because God initiated the idea. The only real guarantee you have is that He will never leave you or forsake you. That means you are not adventuring on your own. You are teamed up with the most powerful being in the universe, and He is on your side.

So why bother doing new things when there is a risk that it may not turn out as you expect? There are many reasons, but let me mention just three. The first is that it is entirely possible that your risk will turn out phenomenally well and that you will learn more about God, yourself, and teaching than you ever thought you would. It is entirely possible that the risk you take will result in a breakthrough that you and your students have been praying for. It is entirely possible that the thing you learn on the journey of taking this risk is the very thing that will open up a whole new world of possibilities for you personally and professionally. In short, taking a risk says we are not satisfied with what we already have and that we know there is more of Him available to us. The possibilities that taking the plunge opens up make the risk worthwhile.

The second reason is simply that faith pleases Him (Hebrews 11:6). When you look fear square in the face and realize that what you are about to undertake has a risk, but you are willing to do it anyway, you please the Father's heart. You are, in effect, saying, "I don't know how this is going to turn out, but I trust that God is going to be with me, and that is enough." Risk asks the question,

"Do I trust Him more than I trust myself?" He always wants more for us. More peace, more love, more understanding. His heart is that we continually grow in our relationship with Him and access all that He has for us. The walk of faith is the place of ever-growing relationship.

Risk asks the question,

"Do I trust Him more than I trust myself?"

The third is this: God says that He wants to give you life—in abundance (John 10:10). We are called to be content but never satisfied with how much of Him we have or know. There is always so much more that He has for us. Ephesians describes it as more than we can ask or think or imagine. I can think and imagine really big, but His desire for me personally, and for every area that I touch, is greater than my capacity to contemplate. That means He has strategies beyond what I can imagine, miracles for me beyond what I can imagine, and peace for me beyond what I can imagine. If all this is available, then why I am not yet walking in it? Because the doorway of access to this great "more" is through faith, aka risk. You choose intentionally (or unintentionally) how much of His presence and power you want to see in your life by choosing how much you are willing to risk in chasing after Him.

All this encouragement to take risks sounds like I am thrill-seeker. I'm not. I am simply a person, like you, who has committed herself to continually seek more of Him and His Kingdom in everything I do. I am in no way saying go out and do dumb stuff for the sake of it. I am saying that a lifestyle of faith is a lifestyle of risk. It never stops feeling a little scary to step beyond the zone where you are comfortable and secure and into the unknown. I encourage you to gather a community around you that will love and support you as you develop further in this lifestyle of risk. As a friend of mine says, "Those who are loved much will risk much." There is something about being in a community where you are taking risks together, challenging one another to go to new heights, celebrating together, and helping one another when things don't go as planned.

I believe that having community around us is critical as we continue on the journey of pursuing God and His Kingdom because we all need a safe place when we fail. "Fail? I'm going to fail?" I hear you cry. Yes, it is inevitable that there will be experiments with the Holy Spirit that will not turn out how you expect. That feels scary to many. We have been trained to fear failure. Somewhere in our lives we got taught that failing at something says something about us. I remember a season when my son really struggled every time he lost any competition, no matter how small. As we talked and prayed together to work out why it was such an emotional experience for him, I realized that he had bought in to the lie that losing said something about him as a person. Every time he lost, he felt that the loss said he was a loser, or that he was not smart, or whatever attribute he associated with that game. In order to train him to think differently, every time I could see him struggling with an impending loss, I would ask him, "What does losing say about you, Ben?" He would frown at me for making him face what he was believing, but I would persist until he answered me. "Nothing! It says absolutely nothing about who I am."

So what does failure try and tell you about yourself? What lie comes against you when you try new things and they don't turn out right? If you have believed that failing makes you a failure, or says that you are not a good teacher, or a good person, then it is no wonder you are reluctant to risk doing new things. It's time to tell the voice of the accuser to back off and start listening to what your good Father says. He delights in your faith. Ask Him how he feels about you and get a Heavenly perspective of the situation. When you have debriefed the experiment, then try telling yourself this truth, "I have just discovered another way not to do this. I am now much wiser and will risk again." "Failure is not fatal" must become our motto if we are to become people of faith.

² "Enlarge the place of your tent,
And let them stretch out the curtains of your dwellings;
Do not spare; Lengthen your cords,
And strengthen your stakes.
³ For you shall expand to the right and to the left,
And your descendants will inherit the nations,
And make the desolate cities inhabited.
⁴ 'Do not fear, for you will not be ashamed;
Neither be disgraced, for you will not be put to shame;
For you will forget the shame of your youth,
And will not remember the reproach of
your widowhood anymore.'"

Isaiah 54:2–4

We are called to be ever enlarging the places of our tents. Notice in the scripture above that God tells us to do the enlarging, and then He will do the expanding. I love how in the same scripture, He addresses the things that might hold us back. He says, "Don't fear, you're not going to be ashamed again. The things that didn't go right in the past don't need to hold you back from your future." He is with you, He is for you; there is more of His help available to you than you have ever imagined. Knowing that He is with you, will you take Him by the hand and seize the opportunity to bring more of His Kingdom into your classroom?

HOW TO GET THE MOST OUT OF THIS BOOK

Understand the Six Components of Each Chapter

Real Life Stories: This first section is the story of how this tool came to be used by the author of that chapter. You will hear honest accounts of the need that presented itself to the teacher and some of the process they took. You will see how God helped meet that need with a tool to bring His Kingdom—one that ultimately got added to the author's toolbox. Here is where you see the tool implemented in Bethel Christian School and the effect of the tool on a classroom.

Summary: The summary provides further understanding of the key components of the tool and the underlying Kingdom Principle on which it is built. The summary will also introduce you to some of the beliefs that you will need to have in place to wield the tool effectively.

Key Mindsets: This gives a list of mindsets that we consider key to the tool being used successfully. It is somewhat of a checklist to see if your beliefs are in alignment with the Kingdom in this area. The key points are written as declarations so you can use them to assist you in reinforcing good mindsets.

Making It Real: This is where it gets down to the nitty-gritty. Here we unpack the tool and talk about what you need to make it work in your environment. We look at different ways to do things, other ideas that enhance the tool, and what you will need to believe to walk it out.

Questions: These questions are designed to get to the heart of the matter. Taking time to process these questions with the Lord is a key to bringing real change. The key to bringing change in your classroom is you, and you are truly changed when you change the way you believe. Don't rush through this section in order to "get on with it." The first part of change is assessing where you are and what you believe. When you have found the answers to the questions and worked through those with God, you are ready to bring real, lasting change to your environment.

Different Ways to Read This Book

Read it right through to get an overview of the book and an initial feel for the tools.

Read it slowly, answering the questions and processing as you go. Introduce the tools as you work through the book.

Read the chapters as you need them for a specific need in your classroom.

Read the book with a friend(s) or colleague(s) and work through the chapters together, forming a support structure for change as you go.

HEAVEN, WE HAVE A PROBLEM
Partnering with the Holy Spirit for Lesson Plans

SARA RUST

To this day, I still remember sitting in a movie theater watching my favorite scene from *Apollo 13*. Radio silence kept NASA's mission control in suspense. Night and day, the men and women on the ground had worked to help the three-man mission return safely home after life-threatening problems arose like clockwork on the capsule. Then finally—they heard the sound of life. Mission control erupts with joy at the audio confirmation that the space capsule had landed safely in the ocean. I have yet to watch this moment with a dry eye.

This nail-biting journey was an incredible saga of problem solving and teamwork, one I still marvel at today. Houston was a lifeline for Apollo 13, supporting the astronauts with ingenuity and guidance to help them return home. As a teacher, I've had my share of *Houston-we-have-a-problem* school days. In fact, if I'm being honest, *most* days it would be nice to have a little *educational* NASA to help direct me with classroom management, differentiation, or designing a lesson plan.

But the truth is—who needs a *Houston* when we have a *Heaven?* God knows. He knows all the requirements and standards you are called to meet. He knows the nuances of your life and schedule and what time you have to plan and prepare. And He knows how he has crafted you and all the students in your class to learn and grow. He is the perfect and most complete resource and manual for problem solving and teaching. In short, NASA has nothing on Jesus.

He is the perfect and most complete resource and manual for problem solving and teaching.

Most teachers recall that the first years of teaching are a blessed mix of epiphany and catastrophe, and it's here in the steep learning curve of firsts that I began calling on the mission control known as Heaven. I recall one science lesson I hadn't spent much time planning for in the midst of everything else going on that week. It was to be a hum-drum but safe lesson of reading the textbook and answering some questions. I remember getting up that morning thinking about the lesson and talking to the Lord about it. I told Him I wasn't that excited about teaching it—that not only would it be boring for all of us, it wasn't really getting to the heart of the reading comprehension skills that I wanted to bolster in my class. As I did my hair and makeup that morning, I just stood on the promise that if it's important to me, it's important to Him. It might have seemed like a silly thing for God to concern Himself with, but I'm convinced our Father delights in us experiencing His Kingdom—and His presence, whenever we can (Luke 12:32).

I was off to school with no new ideas of how to adapt my lesson, but a sneaking suspicion that God's faithfulness would meet me in the journey. Truly, God is always on time, and about five minutes before my science lesson was to begin, Heaven made contact.

Heaven: We're going to turn this science lesson into a game, Ms. Rust. Over.

Ms. Rust: Roger that. Waiting for directives.

Heaven: Pass out packets of science reading as planned. Over.

Ms. Rust: (Hearing class outside door) Roger.

Heaven: Pass out a dry erase board to each table with one marker. Over.

Ms. Rust: (Class is entering taking their seats) Roger that, Heaven.

Heaven: Alrighty. Here's the game plan. Each table is going to read the packet. You are going to ask a series of questions. Each table will write the answer to the question in a complete sentence on their board. Spelling counts. They must tell you where they found the information in the packet to get credit. Any table with the correct answer gets a point.

Ms. Rust: (Already explaining game to class) Got it.

Heaven: Also—we're going to add a little humor to the game. Grab some of the hats from your costume box. Have every table pick a hat and the person from each table who answers the question must stand with hat on head. They'll love it.

Ms. Rust: (Smiling and explaining) Okay, You bet.

Game begins, and students are enthused and ready. But excitement of game has stirred up the class, and it is hard to ask questions over talking populous.

Heaven: Ms. Rust you are cleared for taking penalty points at your discretion. If a group's too loud, or leaning back on their chairs, or being bad sports, just erase a point. That should take care of the noise level.

Ms. Rust: Awesome. Yes! It's working!

Game concludes in perfect timing, with smiling faces all around.

Heaven: Nice work, Ms. Rust. Just to review—this mission covered skills in reading comprehension, inference, attention to detail, sourcing information, grammar, spelling, teamwork, and science content. So glad to help you meeting the needs of your beautiful ESL students who felt included and empowered by their teams. Your movers got to move, your academically minded got to lend their strength to their teams, your competitive students loved the game, while your non-competitive students loved the fact that that points could be earned by all teams after every question. Your quieter students appreciated the order that came from taking the penalty points. And everyone loved wearing bonnets, berets, and sombreros during science class. Love partnering with you.

Here for you, always. Over.

Ms. Rust: Roger that.

As a teacher, of course, it is good practice to be prepared, and I still plan lessons. But I am learning to try to let open communication with God be part of the process. I invite Him to show me how to teach. Sometimes He will inspire me with unit plans or projects months in advance. But often, as I listen for His voice, He will speak in the moment. I have been in the midst of teaching, many times, and ideas will begin to fill my mind—as if I'm receiving a "download" from mission control. Suddenly I have words and strategies that work with my students. These are my favorite moments of teaching, when I am listening to my Father and team teaching with His Spirit.

His Word is our ever-present treasure trove of wisdom.

The key to partnering with the Holy Spirit is learning how *you* hear His voice. Jesus says we can recognize His voice (John 10:27). Do you know how the Father speaks to you? Does He speak through stories or music, or conversations with friends? Do pictures trigger new thoughts and ideas? Maybe you hear best when you go for a walk or take a hot bath. Perhaps you are filled with vision when you research online. And, of course, His Word is our ever-present treasure trove of wisdom. I believe the God who promises to never leave or forsake us is delighted and excited to partner with us in the classroom. He is ready to help. He is willing to speak. He has created you to hear. By faith, you never have to teach alone again. The fullness of heaven has your back.

Roger that?

SUMMARY
Partnering with the Holy Spirit for Lesson Plans

We are not alone. Heaven does want to help. Whether you have planned ahead or are flying by the seat of your pants, the Holy Spirit has some upgrades available for your lesson plans. He wants to partner with you to teach your students in the most effective way possible, and that might mean some changes in the way you do things. Partnering with the Holy Spirit and letting Him in on the lesson planning means you will need to position yourself to listen to Him. Sometimes that inspiration will come in a fleeting thought that must be teased out to become a new lesson or way of doing things. Other times the Holy Spirit will give you a detailed plan before or during your class for what the lesson will look like. Your job is to develop your listening skills and respond by partnering with what He says. It will take courage to risk doing things you have never done before, but the benefits you and your students will uncover will be more than worth it.

KEY MINDSETS

- God is my Mission Control; He wants to help me.

- I can easily hear His voice.

- Partnership with God always leads to increase.

- I love to partner with the Holy Spirit to bring upgrades to my lesson plans.

MAKING IT REAL

God is creative and loves to share His creative ideas with us as we intentionally partner with Him. In this chapter, Sara got her lesson plan on the go, in the middle of a lesson. The Holy Spirit loves to give you "downloads" at a moment's notice wherever you are, but He also loves it when you intentionally ask Him to be a part of your planning time. Take a moment before you start your planning to ask Him what He wants to show you about this lesson. Ask Him for new ideas and to upgrade your old ones. He knows each student in your class, how they learn and what they need to succeed, so trust that He has ideas that will meet your class right where they are.

Sometimes the greatest challenge is our own competence.

Sometimes the greatest challenge is our own competence. Perhaps you have been teaching for a number of years and have your lesson plans well organized and laid out for the year. You know how successful those lessons have been in the past and have no need to change anything. Your competence can lead you to become comfortable to the point that you no longer need the Holy Spirit to come and help you with your planning or your lessons. But there is always more. The Holy Spirit always has a plan on how to adapt your lesson more fully to your current class. You have never taught this lesson to this class in this season before. God wants to help you to continue to grow in excellence, and He has just the ideas that you need to capture your students and bring them to new levels.

If God wants to help you, how do you access that help? Many times we think that our inspirational moments have to be in our "quiet time" with the Lord. He does love to speak to us during those moments we set aside to draw near to Him, but we need to recognize that He loves to speak all the time and will use everything around you. I find that some of my most profound revelations come when I am not thinking about work things at all. He ambushes me with His creative ideas when I am in the garden or walking with my family or even just doing the dishes. Become aware of the times and places that you find most inspirational or where you have met Him before. Intentionally invite more of His presence into those times. Expect Him to speak while you are in the shower, walking the dog, doing the dishes, or on your way to work as well as in your focused time with Him.

Make it a habit to ask the Holy Spirit during your day for input into your lessons. Realize that He is like an ever-present teacher's aide that is longing to download creative ideas and strategies for teaching. He is the expert on the students in your class and has thousands of years of experience in working with people. His list of creative ideas is endless, and He knows your personality and experience and what will work for you. Who wouldn't want to have that kind of partner in their classroom to help them grow and change as a teacher?

He is the expert on the students in your class and has thousands of years of experience in working with people.

Growing in this kind of relationship is like forming any new habit. At first it is a challenge, but it becomes easier with practice. When you start a new way of doing things, the easiest way to remember is to link the new habit with an old one. Maybe you will put up a reminder to ask Him for help while you brush your teeth each morning, or while you drive to school. Maybe walking the dog gives you a chance to quiet yourself and call on His help. In the classroom you can put a sticky note where you will see it as you begin to start a new lesson to help you remember to ask Him for ideas. Put visual reminders around the class that may mean nothing to your students but that remind you that the Holy Spirit is there just waiting to help. He will speak to you, so don't forget to thank Him when you get revelation.

Once He has spoken to you, whether a full-fledged plan or just a fleeting glimpse of an idea, you now need to act on it. Any time we do something new, it can feel a little scary. Remember the first time you ever a taught a lesson on your own? I bet you were a little nervous. You planned it, got your resources ready, and then you just had to do it, no matter how scared you felt. It doesn't feel comfortable to be new at something, so you can expect it to be uncomfortable as you go on an adventure with God in doing new things in your classroom. When the benefits seem small and the risk seems high, take time to remember other ways that embracing risk and following God's lead has led to breakthrough. Celebrate His faithfulness and choose to follow Him again.

QUESTIONS FOR ACTION

- How does God want to help you with your lesson plans?

- How can you include Holy Spirit more in your planning?

- How and where do you hear Him best?

- How can you make more room in your life to hear Him speak?

- What is stopping you from partnering with the Holy Spirit in a greater way in your lesson plans?

- What is God talking to you about personally that He wants to spill over into your class?

2

VICTORY IN THE UNSEEN REALM
Intentionally Changing the Atmosphere with Your Class

JANINE MASON

Have you ever walked into a room and felt tension or anger even though the people in the room have smiles on their faces and everything looks normal? That is because the spiritual atmosphere in the room has been charged by the people who are in it. Maybe the people in the room had a fight before you walked in and said angry words to one another. Their words, the state of their heart, and their actions set up an atmosphere that you experience without ever knowing what went on.

Who we are and the anointing that we carry on our lives is released into the atmosphere around us.

Who we are and the anointing that we carry on our lives is released into the atmosphere around us. This works both in the positive and negative. We can charge our atmosphere with frustration and anger by what we are carrying inside us, or we can charge it with peace, love, and His presence. Equally, the students in our class

31

contribute to the spiritual atmosphere that resides in our class by what they carry and what they intentionally release.

You are ultimately responsible for the atmosphere in your class and can determine what it will be, but teaching your students to manage it with you has a number of benefits. Firstly, it's a numbers game. Instead of there being one teacher actively working to keep the atmosphere sweet and 25 students doing whatever, suddenly there is the potential for 26 people to be working together to invite a great atmosphere. Secondly, we see this as a skill that will help our students throughout their lives. Imagine what our kindergarteners will be doing by age 20 if they learn now that they can manage their atmosphere. I am waiting for the day when parents come to us and say, "My first grader just taught our family to change our atmosphere because they didn't like the one we had."

Whatever they let in then gets to manifest, or show up, in actions.

As we learned the process of working with the unseen realm, God gave me a visual picture to help the kids understand what was going on. We taught them that they are a gateway to let spiritual things into the atmosphere. As the gateway, they get to choose what they let into the atmosphere around them. They can let in love, peace, and all things wonderful, or they can let in anger, resentment, or unforgiveness. Whatever they let in then gets to manifest, or show up, in actions. When they choose to partner with resentment or anger, they let it into the atmosphere around them, and others will be affected by it if they are not aware of what is going on. Alternatively, they can let the good things of God in through their gateway. They can choose to actively invite love and peace into the atmosphere and feel the benefit of that.

Here's how it works. We taught our students that they are a gateway. This gave them a visual image to go with what we were doing. Even a kindergartener knows that a gateway lets things in or keeps things out. We told them that they have power to determine what comes into their classroom by the words they speak and the way they act. We asked them if they had ever felt a "yucky" atmosphere in the class. We asked them to identify what things made the atmosphere nasty. They easily identified things such as anger and grumpiness. Next we asked them to identify how it made them feel with those things in operation. Once we had established that an unpleasant atmosphere was not what we wanted in our class, we asked them what we did want in the atmosphere. They responded with words such as peace, kindness, and love.

Next we talked about how to invite those things into our class. There are many ways to open the gate to God's presence and the attributes that come with Him. Worship, thanksgiving, prayer, acts of kindness, and prophetic acts all change the atmosphere pretty quickly. We also pointed out that we can make declarations that simply invite peace or love or kindness to come into the class. With our younger students, we had them act this out.

We demonstrated being the gateway to them. Two adults held their hands together, acting like a gate. We invited each student to approach the gate, taking on an attribute. As they did, we asked them, "Who are you?" We would then ask the other students if they wanted that attribute in their class. If it was peace, love, or some other attribute found in God's presence, we swung the gate open wide and invited them in. If it was some sort of ugly attribute such as anger, impatience, or fear, we simply said "Stop, you can't come in here."

Even our youngest students got the idea quickly. We gave different students the opportunity to be the gate and reinforced that each of us is a gateway and has power to decide what gets into the class. Teachers followed up the idea with other opportunities to be a gate and to make declarations over their classrooms. Students learned that if peace is lacking in the atmosphere, they can simply turn their face to Heaven and invite peace to come.

Students learned that if peace is lacking in the atmosphere, they can simply turn their face to Heaven and invite peace to come.

This has become normal language for us as a family. I can now simply tell the kids that they have polluted the atmosphere and require them to clean up their mess and make the atmosphere sweet again. A while ago, though, it was me who needed to do the sorting out. My husband was away on a ministry trip for a week or so, and the garage door opener had decided not to work. I warned kids not to open the garage door, as I was not sure I could get it closed again.

One day about three or four days before he was due back, my daughter opened the garage door. We were on our way out to go somewhere fun and had been singing crazy songs together as we got ready. I walked out the front door and found the garage door open. I was angry. I had told them not to touch it, and here it was open. The more I tried to close it, the angrier I got. By now I was thinking that we couldn't go anywhere for three days because of all the stuff in the garage that could be stolen (as I tell my kids, anger makes your brain turn off). After ten minutes or so of grumbling angrily and tugging at the door, I finally got it closed and we piled into the car to go on our happy adventure. Only there weren't any happy kids in there anymore. There was no more singing, just a horrible feeling and no joy. I had messed up big time!

"Hey you guys," I said, "I'm sorry. I was scared we wouldn't be able to go anywhere and I got stressed. I messed up our atmosphere, so I am going to take responsibility to fix it." Now I don't necessarily recommend you do what I did next. But for some crazy reason, I just started singing the first line of the ridiculous song we had been singing together before I got mad. It was so unexpected and so crazy that we couldn't help but laugh, and the atmosphere changed in a moment.

Sometimes it is going to take more than you telling a joke. Sometimes you are going to need a strategy from Heaven to change that atmosphere, but there is always a way for you to invite the atmosphere of Heaven into your environment.

SUMMARY

Intentionally Changing the Atmosphere with Your Class

The atmosphere in our classrooms greatly impacts how our students feel during class and therefore how well they will learn. Because the atmosphere is generally unseen, it is easy to be unaware of it or to feel like we are a victim to its influence. The reality is that God has given us the power to shift the atmosphere to one that resembles the Kingdom of God. Many of us know the promise that God gives to Joshua as he starts his journey into the Promised Land. He tells Joshua clearly, "Every place that the sole of your foot will tread upon I have given you, as I said to Moses" (Joshua 1:3).

---

*Every place you go becomes a place
that you have dominion over.*

It is easy for us to think that this was something specific to Joshua, that it was only for him in that time and place. The truth is that God gives us the same promise today. Every place you go becomes a place that you have dominion over. Does that mean you own every piece of land you step on? No, but it does mean that the spiritual realm in that place is subject to you as a son or daughter of the King.

KEY MINDSETS

- I have been given authority in the unseen realm.

- I set a Heavenly atmosphere in my classroom.

- I can invite my students to partner with me for change.

- Empowering students to change the atmosphere gives them a skill for the future.

- Students can also learn how to control/affect the atmosphere.

- Changing the atmosphere is fun and an essential tool for classroom management.

MAKING IT REAL

The Bible says that we are spirit, soul, and body (1 Thessalonians 5:23). Most people today would agree that we have a soul and a body, but many are unaware of the spiritual realm despite the fact that it impacts us in a very real way. This chapter addresses the need to become aware of the spiritual realm and take ownership of it as a tool to creating a healthy classroom. Though your students may not believe in the unseen realm, they can be trained to recognize what they are sensing from that realm and address it.

The first part of this equation, as always, is you. You have been given authority over all the enemy's power (Luke 10:19), you are born of God and have been given power to overcome the world (1 John 5:4-5), and the One inside you is greater than he who is in the world (1 John 4:4). This is incredible news, particularly on those days when it all seems too much to cope with. You—the Bible makes it very clear—are the one in your classroom who gets to determine what the atmosphere will be. It doesn't matter who comes into your classroom, it doesn't matter what they bring with them, it doesn't even matter whether you feel spiritual or not. What matters is that the Christ (the anointing) who lives inside of you gives you the power to determine what kind of atmosphere resides in your classroom.

You are the one in your classroom who
gets to determine what the atmosphere will be.

What is an atmosphere and how do you change it? When we are talking about the atmosphere in a classroom, we are talking about what has been given power in the unseen realm. When you stand up in the authority you have been given by God, anything in the unseen realm that is against God must bow the knee. The question isn't whether or not you have been given the authority; the question is do you know that reality in the core of your being, and will you actually stand up into that authority and enforce the rule of the Kingdom? You have been set as the guard over your classroom. Your administrators have empowered you to be the leader of that domain, and God has equipped you to be effective in bringing His Kingdom in that place. The Bible says that you have already been given everything you need to lead a Godly life (2 Peter 1:3). It is not something you need to pray and ask for; you already have all that you need at your disposal to establish His Kingdom, the atmosphere of Heaven, in your classroom.

You have been set as the guard over your classroom.

I probably just made you a little nervous. You may internally be comparing how the atmosphere feels in your classroom to the beautiful atmosphere that is established in Heaven, and you realize you don't stack up when compared to Him. It's okay. We are all on a journey where the goal is not perfection, but constant growth. We move from glory to glory as we know Him and who He made us to be in greater dimensions. Let your goal in this area be a partnership with Him where you intentionally grow an atmosphere that is known for His attributes in your classroom.

I am on that same journey, and I have discovered that when I pray and become aware of the truth in any given area, it starts to move from the unseen realm into something that is tangible. So what does that actually look like? In a particularly busy and potentially overwhelming season, I have been drawing the peace of God around me. His word says He gives me peace that surpass-

KINGDOM TOOLS FOR TEACHING

es understanding (Philippians 4:7), so I have decided to become aware of the peace that is available to me despite the un-peaceful circumstances I find myself in. As I have focused on His peace, I have found enough peace for me and for the others around me. I take time throughout the day to momentarily pause and become aware of peace when pressure comes against me. As I have done this, a number of people have given me feedback that when I come into a room, they feel an increased level of peace.

As I have focused on His peace, I have found enough peace for me and for the others around me.

I can't emphasize enough that your belief about the reality of the spiritual realm and your power in it will determine how you experience this realm. I urge you to experiment with the Holy Spirit in growing your awareness of and practicing your authority in your classroom. You are not a victim to the unseen realm. You are made to rule that realm, even in your classroom, where your students bring in all sorts of atmospheres with them. You get to determine the atmosphere through prayer, declaration, worship, and walking in right beliefs.

The second part of this equation is inviting your students to participate with you in establishing the atmosphere in your classroom. How, you may be asking, can I get a bunch of unsaved kids to impact the atmosphere and build the Kingdom with me? I'm glad you asked. The Kingdom of God is the place where He reigns, as evidenced by His nature being expressed. His Kingdom shows up in love (1 John 4:8), in righteousness, peace, and joy (Romans 14:17), and in hope (Jeremiah 29:11). While many students—and for that matter, staff—at your school may not know or want to know Jesus; they do want to experience what is found in His Kingdom. And God is willing for them to experience His attributes so they can get to know Him. Romans 2:4 lets us know that it is the goodness or kindness of God that leads us to repentance. Many times we are trying to get people to repentance so they can know His goodness instead of the other way around. Let His Presence show up in a tangible way, and people suddenly find themselves drawn to the person who brings that sense of peace, love, and hope.

Let His Presence show up in a tangible way, and people suddenly find themselves drawn to the person who brings that sense of peace, love, and hope.

No matter the state of your students, it is possible to get them to ask for His attributes to show up. A teacher in a public school in California shared with me how her students needed help (peace) to settle down after recess. She decided to get her students on board with managing her atmosphere, and here is what happened.

Coming in from their break, many of my students are already hyped up from recess. So before we come in, I ask a student what we do when we come inside. The response, "We ask peace to come into the classroom so we can calm down so we can listen and learn." I tell them to go to their seats and put their heads down while I have the calming music playing. The calming music is an instrumental worship CD. And I pat each one gently on the back, praying for them silently. We do this for about three to five minutes. My principal likes that I have my students calm down after we come in from recess.

Every student has the potential to recognize a nasty atmosphere and know that he or she wants a different one. Simply initiate a discussion about how it feels when it is nasty and how they would like it to feel. Then talk about what kinds of things they would like in their atmosphere. You don't have to use the word *atmosphere*. You can ask them, "How would you like it to feel in here?" or "What kinds of things make you feel safe and ready to learn?" When you have identified what you want to have in your class, talk to the students about how they have the power to invite those kinds of attributes in or to keep other things out. Make a class agreement about the things you want to invite in and the things you want to keep out. Now practice inviting good things in and have your students notice the change in atmosphere. Maybe you will train them to invite peace like the teacher in the testimony above. Maybe you need love to show up. Ask your students to imagine love as a person, and ask them to invite that person in. Jesus will be delighted to show up as the Prince of peace or the God of love.

QUESTIONS FOR ACTION

- What key elements are in the atmosphere of God's Kingdom?

- What atmosphere tends to reign in your classroom?

- What do you believe about your role to set the atmosphere in your classroom?

- Who has authority to set the atmosphere in your classroom?

- How can you train students to recognize and intentionally contribute to the atmosphere of the classroom?

- What challenges you in setting a Godly atmosphere in your class? What beliefs need to change in you to see an outward change?

- How can you invite students to manage their own atmosphere?

- What does your "gateway" let into your classroom each day? What does God want to release into your classroom this week through you?

LOVE BLASTS
Seeing Others From Heaven's Perspective

LINDSAY BROWN

I have these little buckets. They are catch-alls. Some catch the nubby ends of well-worked pencils, others are collectors of the misfit crayons left for peril on the floor, and some hold an altogether different classroom treasure, student names. We teachers call on these name sticks (your ordinary, run-of-the-mill popsicle sticks) for many functions: making groups, finding reluctant helpers, choosing jobs, and of course always choosing fairly. If there's a complaint, we blame it on the name stick. In some instances, children cringe when the name sticks appear. In the honey hive (my kindergarten classroom), a particular calm comes over my students. Are you curious what might bring a hush to the most active zone in an elementary school? Would you believe me if I told you it was kindness?

My buckets all serve a purpose, but I especially love my heart bucket. Inspired by a particularly crazy day with name-calling, unkind accusations, and a heaviness not fit for a kindergarten classroom, the heart bucket came into existence. I grabbed our heart bucket with all my sweet honeybees' names, walked confidently to the front of the classroom, and waited to see who was watching. There's always one watching. I thanked them for their attention, praising them for their leadership, and immediately I had all eyes—and most of the attention. My special heart bucket was the real focus. "Whose name will it be this time?" I could practically hear them all thinking! Pulling one name out of the bucket, I patted our "share chair" next to me and invited my student to sit. Looks of confusion and uncomfortable giggles spread across the class. *What is this crazy lady up to now?"* I'm sure was what they were all thinking.

As my student situated himself on the chair, seemingly waiting for the worst, I invited the other kindergarteners to think of something special about this student. They could think of something they'd noticed and use it in an encouraging word, or they could ask God for a special word about what He sees and thinks. I could feel the relief and confusion; "A kind word, for this guy?" The student I chose from the heart bucket was a purposeful choice. He is an atmosphere shifter, a game changer, but the game was not going in our favor that day! We needed a change up. What better way to shift the atmosphere? It was time to go mining for gold. God bless my kindergarteners, and praise the Lord for Holy Spirit-inspired moments.

At Bethel Christian School, we are gold diggers.
We choose to mine the goodness that God has
placed in our students and our peers.

At Bethel Christian School, we are gold diggers. We choose to mine the goodness that God has placed in our students and our peers. At times this can be a challenge, when all that can be seen are the frustrating behaviors and the day-to-day difficulties. Most often the things that change the climate in a classroom are the beautiful gems just waiting to be discovered. As teachers we have the distinct honor of inviting our students to participate in this treasure hunt. We are the leaders of this classroom revolution!

As teachers we have the distinct honor of inviting our students to participate in this treasure hunt. We are the leaders of this classroom revolution!

The first time my class experienced a love blast was the last time they dreaded the bucket of names. Seeing from the eyes of kindness changed quite a few things in my classroom. The frustrating behaviors and day-to-day difficulties didn't disappear, but my students were discovering that their words were powerful. Powerful enough to bring peace where there once was chaos, understanding where accusations and unkindness tried to destroy friendship. Our words are a force that can bring life or death. My kindergarteners were learning first hand Proverbs 18:21, "Death and life are in the power of the tongue." Instead of hurling insults and unkind names, my students were throwing love blasts: bursts of kindness to bless and build up.

Love blasts are just one way you can shift the atmosphere in your class with kindness. I have found for my age group that this is a great visual, but it also involves whole class participation. They are eager to give an encouraging word or share a kindness with their classmate. After each encouragement is spoken, the whole class responds with the phrase "LOVE BLAST!" It's solidarity and a way of saying "I agree." Students have all different levels of words that pour out: "You are a good friend." "I like your shirt." "You are God's favorite." Every word is honored and followed by a love blast. The most surprising part for me as a teacher is seeing my students excited not just to receive but also to give a love blast.

Setting the standard for kindness in your class is an inside job. You get to determine the level of invitation you want to offer your students. The class that brought about the love blasts was a particularly challenging group of students and demanded something more from my arsenal of teacher artillery. Love blasts were a momentary inspiration from the Holy Spirit that brought about change in my classroom. You may find that your classroom needs a different invitation to the same kindness party. The goal is to give students the opportunity to see each other through the lens of good.

The goal is to give students the opportunity to see each other through the lens of good.

No matter what environment you are called to, kindness always wins. The most important part of the love blast process is exposure. I love the idea of affirmation mailboxes, gold/honey pots of kind words, anything that gives students an opportunity to share kind words with their peers. These are great ideas and are also key to creating an atmosphere of love and appreciation. Love blasts are meant to provide an opportunity for the whole class to see what others may not automatically see about another student. This exposure draws all students into the process.

SUMMARY
Seeing Others From Heaven's Perspective

The simple act of speaking out kind words to one another has the power to change the atmosphere in our classrooms. It can take a classroom that feels full of antagonism and change it to one where people feel known and celebrated.

All of us, particularly when we are having a bad day, can fall into the trap of looking at the negative in people. When we train our students to intentionally look for the good in others and speak those things out as kind words, we are setting up the atmosphere in our classroom to be one where students actually want to be.

It starts simply with a choice, by you, to see the best in every student, even on their worst day. When you choose to set your heart to see the best, to see the gold in them, you are setting yourself up to see through His eyes. It begins with your ability to choose to see this way consistently and then by leading your class in learning to do the same. By choosing to focus on the positive as a community, you are creating a safe place, a place where the beauty of each student is put on display and celebrated with words.

KEY MINDSETS

- There is always something good to see in every student.

- Speaking kind words brings me into agreement with God and changes the atmosphere.

- I lead my students in seeing and speaking the best about others.

- I show grace to every student because I have experienced God's kindness.

MAKING IT REAL

Everyone has a great need to feel known and to be celebrated for who they are. When Lindsay introduced love blasts to her kindergartners, it was in response to one of those days when kids were being kids. We've all had those days when everyone seems to be on edge, and everyone seems to only see the worst in the people around them. It starts with a few quiet comments, and pretty soon it can feel like an all-out war zone in your classroom. You can soothe the ruffled feathers one on one, or you can invite your class into the process by teaching them to change the atmosphere by looking for the good in their classmates.

Here's what it is going to take: first, you are going to have to deal with your own "lens" through which you see the students in your class. Maybe you start every year with the hope that each and every student will be an angel all year long. (Yeah right!) You only have to be there a short time before you are reminded that some of your students are CHALLENGING, and challenging is code for what you really want to say about them. They seem to want to take your day and turn it upside down. It can feel like some really have it in for you. You wonder to yourself, "How did I become the bad guy?" Your wonderful belief about your class that you started the year with can go downhill fast if you don't keep your lens closely aligned with Heaven's view.

Having your students look for the best in one another starts with you.

Having your students look for the best in one another starts with you. It is easy to see the difficult behavior when you are the one who has to deal with it day after day, but that student you are struggling with is more than just bad behavior. He or she is a bundle of God-given talent and giftedness. That beauty may not be on display, but if you will take the time to dig for the gold, you will find it. Seeing, really seeing, this beauty is what enables you to lead your class in digging right along with you for the things there are to celebrate.

It's a choice. You decide how you will see your students. You can see them through the lens of accomplishment, effort, or behavior. When we use these lenses, we naturally tend to rank our students from the best to the worst. The ones at the top end of the behavior scale need little help or adjustment, while those at the other end catch our attention constantly. Our eyes are on them to watch for what they will do next to disrupt the class. We learn to anticipate the bad behavior and "head it off at the pass." This is smart classroom management. It pays to know where trouble is likely to come from. The problem with it is that, unless we guard against it, our lens for those students becomes primarily a lens of watching for the negative behavior.

Instead, each day you will need to align yourself with Heaven's view of those students. Yes there are issues that need to be addressed, but there is also tremendous treasure inside of the student to be dug out. Spend time asking the Lord how He sees that student personally. He or she is not just one of the faceless billions that Jesus died for. They are a beloved child of His, full of potential and known intimately by Him. Take time to ask why some of the challenging behaviors are there. Sometimes they are the result of tremendous brokenness. Grace can come as you understand what that student is facing. Sometimes the very thing that drives you crazy is part of the beauty that they are to bring to the world.

I had a group of parents of middle school students ask the Lord why He gave their student a particular attribute that they found difficult to live with. God showed one mother of an extroverted class clown how he is called to influence many through his personality and demeanor. It totally changed how his mother saw him. What she had seen as exhausting and frustrating, she now saw as a God-given strength to be channeled and used for God. Other parents had similar experiences as they simply took the time to get a fresh view of how Heaven saw their child.

Your students may struggle with some of the same issues relating to the challenging students in your class. Disruptive behavior often affects them as much as it affects you. They are watching you to see how you respond, not just in love blast-type situations, but also throughout the day. Model to them how to focus on the best qualities in others. Help them to look for the best by drawing attention to the positive attributes of those they struggle with. Lindsay led her class in writing kind notes and cards to a student that the whole class was struggling with. This young man's challenging behavior had affected all the students, and they were at a point of being "over it." On a day he was away, they decided to go "gold-mining" and wrote about the good things they found. The young man was blessed that they valued him enough to write cards for him.

Lindsay's love blasts are verbal affirmations of things that students appreciate about their classmates. Other teachers set up a supply of index cards and some sort of letter boxes that students used to drop notes into. Don't forget to add your own notes in there too. Look for opportunities to give your students kind words and for them to speak kindly to their classmates throughout the day. Waiting in line can be a great opportunity to turn to your neighbor and say something kind. As you create a culture of kindness, may your classroom become known as the kindest class in the school.

QUESTIONS FOR ACTION

- What lens do you see your students through?

- How can you maintain God's lens (seeing the good) when a student is consistently difficult to work with?

- How can you model and teach students to use that lens?

- What effect does the lens you use have on the culture of your classroom?

- How does God show kindness to you?

ADVENTURES IN RAISING LEADERS
Empowering Students Beyond Your Comfort Zone

SARA RUST

It all began with one simple problem: I was lonely.

When my first year of teaching had come to a close, I remember my principal asking me if I would be open to leading worship in our K–4th grade weekly chapel the following year. I was an optimist and eager for new challenges. "Sure, I'd be open to that," I replied before really thinking it through (a skill I had perfected unintentionally as a first year teacher). My theoretical "openness" to the idea gently shifted into a full-fledged commitment as the new year began.

And there I stood at our first chapel. A teacher alone on the stage with her guitar, staring at hundreds of little faces, realizing at that moment I actually had no idea what I was doing. How do I teach these little ones about worship? How do I lead them into encounters? Do they understand any of these songs we're singing? How do I play B minor again? Could someone tune my guitar? Why did I sign up for this? Can someone get me a coffee?

The first few weeks, I sheepishly made my way to the empty stage. I was used to leading adults in worship, but elementary students were a whole new ballgame. It didn't take long before the loneliness of standing on that stage with just my trusty six-string prompted me to consider the idea of starting a band. It's just that people who start bands always seem so inherently hip to me. And I didn't feel I had enough swag to rope in an egg shaker.

One day while teaching, I was in negotiation talks with God about how I couldn't continue to lead worship alone. Unless He provided a band, I was going to drop this gig. At that moment, He encouraged me to look around my classroom at the third and fourth grade students sitting at the tables. "There's your band," He said. "Invite them to lead with you."

"There's your band," He said. "Invite them to lead with you."

Knowing His ideas always seem to pan out, I agreed to invite them to join me. I began by bringing my guitar to class and teaching them songs. Suddenly a few singers joined me on stage every week. One of our students donated beautiful worship flags to our class. Now our band had a few flaggers and dancers to lead. A boy in the class had a dream of becoming a drummer and was taking lessons. He brought his hand drum to school one day to practice with our class, and suddenly—our band had rhythm! Week after week our class began to grow in leadership and depth as they became the worship team for the elementary school. I was in awe as I watched them lead through song and prayer, whether they were on stage or not.

The following year, our worship team transitioned as some students moved onto junior high and new students joined the ranks of fourth grade. We began a journey of going beyond just learning songs and creating hand motions to spending time listening to God during our practice the day before chapel and getting a "game plan" for our worship time. This generally looked like me standing at the board asking the students to take a few moments and listen to God for words or pictures. I'd ask questions like, "What do you think God wants to do tomorrow? What's on His heart? Is there anything we should be praying about?" Students would share words and pictures that would come to mind, and I would draw or write them on the board. Then as a team, we would look at the board and see if there were any directions or themes that showed up for the following day's chapel.

At one memorable after-school practice, God told me to hand the dry erase marker over to a student to lead this time. I walked to the back of the room and watched a group of ten-year-olds seek heaven together for a strategy on leading the younger students into an encounter with the Living God. The board was covered with pictures and words, and by the end, the students knew the direction they wanted to lead and pray into at chapel the next day. I was in awe of how much they could do as I stood back and watched.

Never underestimate the abilities of a child.

Though there were practical things I taught the teams over the years, it began with the most important step: an invitation. Never underestimate the abilities of a child. Sometimes all children are waiting for is an invitation to step into their God-given greatness.

SUMMARY

Empowering Students Beyond Your Comfort Zone

Our students are far more capable than many of us give them credit for. Often times they are simply waiting for an opportunity and an invitation to step up to the plate and into a role of leadership. "Yeah right," I hear you think. "You don't know my class." I don't know your class, but I do know God. I know that He entrusts me with more power and authority than I deserve. I know He believes in me far more than I believe in myself. I know that He lets me be involved with His work when He could always do it better Himself.

He entrusts me with more power and authority than I deserve.

There is another thing I've noticed about Him. He is not afraid of my messing up and making Him look bad. He is happy to work through my imperfections and my immaturity. I'm not talking about being lax about sin; I'm talking about the fact that I always need to grow more in Him and that compared to Him, I'm just a baby. I've also noticed that He usually empowers me before I think I'm ready. If I want to represent Him well, to be like Him in my interactions with people (even little ones), then I had better be prepared to do the same. I need to empower the people in my life to step up and take ownership of their lives to the fullest extent to which they are capable.

KEY MINDSETS

- God empowers me beyond what I deserve or think I am ready for.

- I don't need to be in control for things to work.

- Failures aren't fatal. It doesn't have to look perfect for God to use it.

- My feelings of discomfort or anxiety do not negate the fact that God is leading me.

- Empowerment brings ownership.

- God uses children/students as powerfully as teachers.

MAKING IT REAL

It's all about empowerment. If you want students to take ownership of their learning, if you want them to be responsible for themselves, then you are going to have to show them that you believe that they are capable of doing just that. The belief that they are powerful human beings, no matter their age, needs to show up in all your interactions with them, not just the ones where it is comfortable. I am not advocating anarchy. I believe in order and in classroom management, but our training on keeping order in our classrooms sometimes prevents us from empowering our students to the extent that they could be empowered. We have been trained that a successful teacher does all the teaching and leads in every area of the class. We encourage our students to serve the class by erasing the board, picking up trash, and leading the line when we move from one space to another, but we rarely give them the message that we believe they have more to offer us than good behavior.

I wonder what would happen if we gave our wiggly kindergartner that can never sit still some input into what our PE lesson looks like. I wonder how he or she would feel about themselves as they stepped into a leadership role by focusing their energy and sharing with the class how to jump rope or throw a ball? I wonder how our budding authors would feel if they had an opportunity to share not only the work they had written but also their process for doing so.

People rise to the level of our beliefs about them.

People rise to the level of our beliefs about them. If I believe that my students are basically people that need to be quiet and receptive to my teaching, but that they have nothing to offer in return, I will experience them as such. But if I believe that every one of them has something to offer to the class, something that they can lead in, then I will discover the best of them and empower them to step into their God-given role. Not every student wants to stand in front of a class and share, but every student has something to offer that needs to be recognized, encouraged, and empowered. Your quietest student may be the class leader of compassion. When a student is struggling with grief, empower them to lead the class in showing kindness and tenderness. Can your math whiz lead a part of the lesson or be given the responsibility of showing others how they work through a problem?

Obviously different ages have different capacities to lead and to manage themselves. It is not wise to give a first grader the same freedom that you would give to a senior in high school, yet both need to know that you trust them to do what they are capable of doing for themselves. When we take away the opportunity to do things for themselves and others, we rob them of their ability to see themselves as powerful people.

Sara, in inviting her students to lead worship with her, had to move past her own desire to have things looking and sounding perfect and trust that God could use the kids in her team to minister as powerfully as she did. Ten-year-olds, you may have noticed, don't generally have the same level of skill as adults do. Their leading worship was never going to be as professional as if an adult team had done it. The temptation is to focus on the fact that we can do everything better than our students simply because we are older and have more experience. When we do this, we miss the opportunity to demonstrate to our students that they have something to offer to one another.

It is one thing to tell students, "You are great, I love what you do," and a whole different picture to show them that we really believe it. When we empower students, we give the whole class a very clear picture that we believe in them as powerful people, able to share their greatness with others. When Sara gathered her team, she also had to put aside her thoughts about what it "should" look like and invite the students into a place of real ownership. She gave up the notion of the music being professional, but she gained a whole lot more. By giving them some room to lead, she got a level of buy-in that was much higher for those students and for the friends they were leading. She demonstrated to the class that she believes that ten-year-olds can manage themselves, can hear from God, and can lead others in what they hear. As she grew her team in their leadership ability, she was telling them through her actions what she had already told them in words: "You are valuable. What you have to offer our class and our junior school is amazing."

I am not suggesting you hand over control of your class and your lessons to the students, but I am inviting you to look for places to give them more ownership of their learning and environment.

Empowering students to be more involved can have numerous expressions. For younger children, it is looking at the jobs that we give them to do and taking them to a new level. For older students, it is looking intentionally for ways to give them the message "I believe you can do it." With all of them, it is looking for opportunities to show them that we trust their ability to manage themselves and to lead others.

For our kindergarten students, it looks like this. They will start the year by saying declarations over themselves, led by the teacher (see the chapter on blessing on brains and bodies). Once they have learned how to do that successfully, the teacher will invite them to help choose what the declarations will be over the class that day. Once they have shown her that they can be trusted, she will then invite a student to lead the class in their declarations for the day. It is powerful to see a five- or six-year-old lead their peers in declaring the truth over themselves. The teacher could do it and know exactly what will be said every time. It's safe and there will be no surprises. Having the student lead is a little risky, but it says to the class that she trusts them to know what needs to be spoken that day. It teaches them that perfection of speech is not the goal; speaking life is. It allows students to take the tool of making declarations to a different level than they would by just following the teacher's lead. This in turn gives the students an ability to use declarations at home and in other areas of their life.

For older students, examine your beliefs about what they are capable of. Many times it is not their lack of ability that stops us empowering them, but our own lack of willingness to lose control. How can you empower them beyond what is normal, and in doing so, invite them into a new level of leadership? Are you doing things for them that they are capable of doing for themselves? How can you see and release the unique greatness of each student to lead in some way in your class?

It can feel uncomfortable to let a student do something at a lower level of proficiency than you.

To empower students to a new level, you are going to have to look at what you believe about being the teacher and about being in control. Your training has taught you to stay in control of the classroom, and it feels safe to do so. It will possibly take a shift in thinking on your part to enable you to empower students in a greater way. It can feel uncomfortable to let a student do something at a lower level of proficiency than you. The benefits of empowerment—to not only that student but the entire class—are worth the risk. Set your students free to step into leadership of themselves and of their peers and watch them come alive to be the best version of themselves.

QUESTIONS FOR ACTION

- How can you empower and activate your students more?

- What fears would hold you back from empowering your students in a greater way? What does God say about those fears?

- What are the benefits of empowering your students?

- What do I believe about things looking messy or out of control?

- What do I believe about my students' ability to lead?

- What is God asking me to entrust to them?

- What can I ask my students to lead this week?

- How can I change my perspective of my students to see them as powerful people?

- What is God's invitation to me? In what area of my life is He entrusting more to me?

A CHANGE OF HEART
Teaching Students the Power of Celebrating Others

LINDSAY BROWN

I have a few words that are not allowed in my classroom. My two least favorite words I hear most often are "no fair." Children are full of justice and what is fair for them. As adults, we inherently know from experience that there are things that are not fair. How do we teach our children to honor, praise, proclaim, and bless when it feels unfair?

Let's be honest; fingernails on a chalkboard aside, the most annoying sound in a classroom is the "awwww" and "no fair" that inevitably comes when children don't get their way. As a teacher I find myself cringing at the "but I wanted" and "that's not fair." No matter how many times they get what they want or more importantly what they need, there's inevitably a "no fair" moment.

As adults we experience this daily. Someone around us may have more than us, or they have what we are longing to have in our lives: that beautiful new home, a fancy new car, financial abundance, the list goes on. I'm sure we can all picture that thing, or things, that we are longing for, maybe even fighting for, and our neighbor next door is living it out. So how do we celebrate others when our hearts are crying "no fair?"

So how do we celebrate others when our hearts are crying "no fair?"

I can remember the moment God asked me this question. I was in the middle of a calendar time, sharing good things with my students. For the umpteenth time, one of my students made the dreaded "awww" at the expense of someone else's joy in having been chosen to share. I was burning up on the inside. Have you ever had that moment with your students? It seems so minor. We could quickly move past these small and seemingly insignificant injustices. Yet, these are the moments that we can begin to develop character and give it language to set our students up for a lifetime of success and celebration. Creating a culture of honor means creating a culture that includes celebration. In this moment, God, ever the gentleman, began whispering to my heart reminders of my own need for celebration in my life.

Creating a culture of honor means creating a culture that includes celebration.

It seems my personal life has glimmers and reflections in my classroom. On this day I was feeling slightly affronted at the reminder I needed to open my own heart for celebration. As I responded to the sting of God's gentle reprimand, it opened up a whole new language and sense of honor in my classroom. Instead of quickly moving past the "no fair" zone, we pressed in to see what God wanted to do. In the presence of the Lord, there is fullness of joy. It was time to get joyful.

I took this as a teaching moment and made myself vulnerable to my class. Is this possible, you might ask, to be vulnerable and real with your students, especially younger ones? Absolutely! There is so much false witness in most of our students' lives. We owe them an encounter with the true and living God, and often that comes through our own (appropriate) vulnerability! Today, we were about to embark on a journey together in learning to celebrate even when our hearts are crying out for equality. I shared with my students, in language they could digest, what I was walking through myself. I explained that some of my friends were having breakthroughs and were getting what I was longing for myself. We talked about how that feels but also what it looks like to cheer on your friends even when they are getting the very thing you long for. I talked about how it was really important to celebrate when somebody gets what you want because we are sharing their joy. I pointed out that one day it is going to be their turn, and they want others to celebrate with them.

At this point my students needed something to frame this pep talk and to make it tangible. We adopted a little song to sing when we want to moan and say it's not fair. We use it to remind ourselves of who we are, that we are a class that celebrates our friends even when it doesn't seem fair. Now, instead of moaning, my students sing this little song of celebration. It's nothing fancy; we just sing the word *celebrate* over and over, and sometimes we celebrate with the sign language for cheering or clapping. The song is simply a reminder that a classroom of honor is a classroom that celebrates one another.

Celebration is not an immediate reaction for this age group, or any age group. Praise and honor are things that have to be taught, modeled, and reinforced. As teachers, we are the ones that both model and reinforce the culture of honor that we want in our classrooms.

Celebration is an inside job that often begins with a choice

Just like honor, celebration is an inside job that often begins with a choice. I can't expect my students to have the immediate desire to praise and cheer on their peers. But they can choose to celebrate their classmates. When my students choose to champion others, peace and joy begin to rule our environment. The result of pressing in and bringing a language of celebration and honor is the foundation of a safe and happy classroom.

Once I had established this culture in my classroom, it was amazing to see how the students reinforced it themselves. One little boy was struggling with the ability to celebrate others. He often wanted to complain when others got what he wanted, but his classmates began to remind him by saying, "Hey, we celebrate in the class." I noticed last week that when someone else got to put a marble in the jar, he was the first one to cheer, and I could see that he was intentionally doing the opposite of what he was feeling. He had changed from a follower to a leader of celebration.

SUMMARY

There are many tiny injustices that happen every day in our classrooms that elicit the "no fair" response from our students, whether verbally or silently. We can manage the outward response or we can take the opportunity to begin to train our students in a different way to think, to have a change of heart. The Bible says to "rejoice with those who rejoice" (Romans 12:15). Most of us, even as adults, have a hard time rejoicing with someone who has what we want. We must train ourselves and our students to adopt a different way of thinking and behaving if we want to abolish the "It's not fair" zone.

This tool is really about establishing a culture of honor as what is acceptable in the classroom. Banning the verbal response that you can hear only goes part way to changing the culture. Instead you need to train your students to have a change of heart, to change the way they see things. They will learn to focus on the good that they have and to intentionally celebrate others.

KEY MINDSETS

- Celebrating others is a weapon to crush comparison and poverty mentalities.

- I choose to rejoice over others' breakthroughs.

- I focus on what I have been given rather than what I still need.

- I choose an attitude of gratefulness in every season.

- When I know the Father celebrates me, it is easy to celebrate others.

- Celebration creates an environment where people thrive and allows students to reach their full potential.

MAKING IT REAL

The goal of this tool is to create a culture of celebration in your classroom where students learn to celebrate the success of others. The outcome will be that students are less likely to play the "It's not fair" card. More importantly it is an internal shift in perspective rather than an external change in behavior. You can get compliance on the outside by setting the standard of behavior and reinforcing it, or you can take the longer route and actually work to shift the way a student sees life. This internal shift may take longer to achieve, but it is the way to set our students up for success. It should be noted that for some students, this may be more difficult, as parents have reinforced the way of thinking by responding and rewarding the "it's not fair" card.

So how do you actually begin to change the way a student responds to others' joy? Firstly initiate a discussion on how it feels to be the one who has something to celebrate. Different age groups will identify with different circumstances that put them in that place. Kindergartners want to be the first to do everything, whereas older students may value high scores on an exam or getting a new possession more highly. Ask the group to identify how it feels to share good news and have others respond negatively. Nobody likes that response, and even young children should be able to articulate to some extent that it reduces their joy when others moan or complain. Part of establishing your class culture is pointing out that "In this class, we choose not to do anything that hurts our classmates." You are going to train your students to take their eyes off themselves and put them onto others. Ask them what they want when they are the ones to be celebrated and make a plan to implement those ideas as part of your classroom culture.

All of us find it more difficult to celebrate others when we are longing for what they have been given. Whether it is the celebration itself or the reason for the celebration, it is hard for us to cheer our friends on when we are acutely aware of our own lack in that area. I remember a time when we had been crying out to God for a new car because ours was dying. A friend, who was in a much better financial position than us, was given a brand-new vehicle at that time. Everything inside me wanted to cry out "It's not fair." Instead I had to turn my attention to all I had been given and be grateful for that. Once I was aware of God's goodness to me, I was in a position to truly celebrate with our friend.

Lack of celebration of others comes out of a poverty mentality. It is the focus on what I don't currently have that makes it difficult to celebrate what others are getting. I've used the following illustration when working with middle school students and adults alike. Ask your students to line up in order of height from tallest to shortest. (Or use a different visible measure if your class is sensitive to the height issue.) Point out that your class is only a small proportion of the world and that the line really continues in both directions. Ask how they arranged themselves and highlight that it was through comparison. Now talk about how it feels to be in different places in the line.

If being tall is the coolest thing, then those further down the line may feel bad about being shorter. People in the middle of the line tend to look at the taller end and want to be there rather than looking down the line and being grateful for where they are. Now suggest some other, more emotionally charged categories of how the class could be sorted. Ask students to think about, but not move to, where they would be in a line if it were arranged by scores on math tests. Some will be fine with that. Others will be horrified at the thought.

Your goal is to help students become aware of the fact that they naturally compare themselves with others all the time and in many different areas. This comparison is going on constantly and usually results in students feeling bad about themselves or lording it over others. They are generally looking up the line and focusing on what they don't have or can't do. When the focus is on what they are lacking, it is hard to celebrate others.

When the focus is on what they are lacking,
it is hard to celebrate others.

Help students see that there are always people further "down" the line than them in some area—if not in their class, then somewhere in the world. We must learn not to compare and focus on what we don't have. Rather, for us to be successful in life, we must see what we have been given and celebrate that. When we can do that, it is much easier to celebrate others.

QUESTIONS FOR ACTION

- How does celebration (or lack of it) shape the atmosphere and culture in your classroom?

- How can you teach your children to honor, praise, proclaim, and bless when it feels unfair?

- In what ways can you create a culture of celebrating others in your classroom?

- How do you respond when someone else gets something you want?

- What does God want to show you about how He celebrates you?

- Think of a time you've been celebrated—how did it feel? Remember that God is celebrating you extravagantly every day.

- What or who is God inviting you to celebrate today?

- What or who is He inviting your class to celebrate today?

6

SOAKING WITH PURPOSE
Training Students to Walk in Peace

TAWNY NOVOSAD

Four years ago, if I had heard that students were soaking in the classroom, I would have automatically assumed it probably wasn't under the teacher's guidance and there was going to be a mess to clean up. Scenes of water blasters and soapy sponges would have automatically danced through my head. I had no grid for any other type of soaking and I didn't approve of water fights in the classroom.

I have since learned that there is another type of soaking that is appropriate and actually beneficial in the classroom. In this type you are to find a quiet space and just sit before the Lord. No writing, no reading, no talking, and no asking questions or petitions of Him. It is an act of worship. Just sit or lay down in the presence of the Holy One, preferably with soft, gentle soaking music playing in the background. It is the very deliberate act of being still, knowing He is God and soaking in His peace, goodness, mercy, love, grace, and kindness. Soaking brings forth encounters, manifestations, and revelation of identities.

I personally experienced soaking for the first time when I went to my initial Bethel Christian School (BCS) training. My roommate asked if it was okay to play soaking music to fall asleep to. Having no idea what she was referring to, I hesitantly agreed. What came out of her IPOD as I began to close my eyes for the night was some of the most beautiful, angelic sounds I had ever heard. My eyes filled with tears and I felt warmth over my entire body. I had some of the most restful, peace-filled slumber I had ever experienced in my life. When we awoke the next morning, I shyly asked her what soaking music was and how could I get my hands on some of it. This new sweet friend and colleague explained to me what soaking in God's presence looked like. She also let me know that in BCS soaking happens in the classroom.

Now that I had discovered soaking, the sort you can do without getting wet, I began to soak in my living room, bedroom, and pretty much anywhere I could. Soaking became my lifeline to heavenly encounters and I couldn't believe it had taken me so many years to begin this part of my journey.

Soaking became my lifeline to heavenly encounters.

When Saul was given over to a tormenting demon in the Old Testament, (1 Samuel 16:14-23) the only thing that would bring him comfort was the music played on the harp or lyre. Every time the tormenting would begin, the harpist (David) would play and it was a physical and spiritual relief for Saul. In the same way, when we soak playing soft and soothing music and put our focus on the Lord, it brings peace and comfort to us.

Having discovered the power of soaking in my personal life it was time to bring it to my classroom. In that season I was having a hard time with a particularly excitable group of students during our second grade math class. I had tried everything to get this group of young, vibrant world changers to sit still and learn math and nothing seemed to work. In desperation I cried out to God for a solution. That's when the Holy Spirit reminded me about soaking in the classroom. I began devoting the first ten minutes of class to soaking, as a way of setting up my class for success. The students would come in and immediately find their soaking spots and we'd dive right in. The atmosphere of our classroom changed drastically and I had students thriving in math as an added bonus!

Rest assured, soaking will bring the Spirit of Peace to your room in a way you never imagined.

You may be wondering how to do this in a class with a room full of giggly, wiggly kids or antsy, bored teenagers. Rest assured, soaking will bring the Spirit of Peace to your room in a way you never imagined. Before ever actually soaking, talk to the class about what soaking is and what it looks like in a classroom. Don Mayer, our wonderful principal, demonstrates this beautifully for our students. He holds up a dry sponge in the shape of a child. He talks about how this child feels dried up and distant from God. He then shares with the students what soaking is and how it is as if you were lying down in the Holy Spirit's water while getting filled up. When he draws the sponge out of the bowl of water, he points to the fact that the sponge is dripping with God's presence. When you are so wet with the glory of God, you can easily drop and splash on everyone around you (he then makes sure to splash a few lucky students in the front row). This is a powerful and memorable picture for young and old. The picture does not have to be associated just with soaking in God's presence. It can just as easy be a picture of soaking in peace. When we are soaked in peace we become easier to work with and we splash that peace over the others around us.

In my personal opinion, there is one thing that makes for successful soaking in a classroom. It is that the teacher soaks as well. Even though it may seem as the perfect time to get materials gathered or respond to that parent email, I assure you nothing compares to the teacher soaking with his or her students. The students are given a wonderful example of what it looks like to soak and it's good for YOU! I am much happier, more relaxed and full of peace and joy when I have had a soaking time with my students. By soaking with them I am demonstrating the importance I place on this activity and showing them through my life the benefits of it. You don't need to close your eyes and lie on the floor for the students to see you joining in. Soaking can look like very quietly and calmly walking round the class and laying hands on students to impart peace. Your students need to see that it is not a work time for you but a time where you are also drawing peace around yourself.

Your students need to see that it is not a work time for you but a time where you are also drawing peace around yourself.

Whether you teach four year olds or eighteen year olds, I encourage you start soaking with them. This important act of quieting yourself during the day is a guaranteed way to bring peace, joy, and connection into your classroom.

SUMMARY
Training Students to Walk in Peace

He is the Prince of Peace and He loves to show up in your classroom and bring His tangible peace with Him. Soaking times allow time for students to connect with the Prince of Peace during the school day, even if they don't know who He is. Remember that although a soaking time is quiet by nature, peace being present during work times isn't necessarily so. As you develop a greater level of peace in your classroom it will change the atmosphere but not necessarily the volume.

The greater the level of peace that you cultivate in your own life and in your classroom the easier it will be to lead your students in this. You may wish to practice soaking at home before you introduce it to your class. Intentionally grow your capacity to become aware of the peace that He gives to you. When you are ready to take this to your class think through the language you will use with them, especially if you are not able to overtly use your soaking time to worship Jesus. Be ready to share with them how learning to walk in a greater level of peace has helped you and how you want to help them learn to do the same.

KEY MINDSETS/DECLARATIONS

- Time spent in worship or setting the atmosphere in a classroom is not wasted time.

- Students who walk in peace learn well.

- The level of peace I carry affects my classroom atmosphere.

- When my students or I invite peace into our classroom we are actually inviting the Prince of Peace to show up.

- I carry and release peace into my classroom.

- God's ability to release peace is greater than my ability to stress out.

MAKING IT REAL

Soaking time does not have to be overt worship time. Where there is freedom to do so by all means have your students focus on Jesus. In other settings you can simply invite peace into your classroom as you rest quietly with instrumental music. Trust that your authority over the classroom sets up an atmosphere that invites His presence. You may wish to lay hands on any students that are struggling and silently release peace over them as you go through this process together. He is the Prince of Peace and loves to show up and bring an atmosphere of peace that is tangible.

He is the Prince of Peace and loves to show up and bring an atmosphere of peace that is tangible.

Part of managing the level of peace in your classroom is managing your own internal peace level.

[6] "Be anxious for nothing, but in everything by prayer and supplication, with thanksgiving, let your requests be made known to God; [7] and the peace of God, which surpasses all understanding, will guard your hearts and minds through Christ Jesus."

Philippians 4:6-7

You have access to peace that surpasses understanding. Even when you seem to have a good reason to be anxious the Bible says to come to God and talk with Him about it. Let go of the challenges, ask Him for what you need and then let His peace reign in you. It sounds easy but when you have challenges going on in your life

81

it can seem so hard. The key is really letting go and trusting God to work on your behalf and getting His perspective on the matter. Once you've connected with Him and have His perspective you are in the place to see that nothing is impossible. When you have His perspective that's when you get access to His peace. I've noticed that no matter what it is that stresses me out, He is not worried, ever.

Make every effort to develop peace as a lifestyle.

I love how the Bible goes on to say that the God kind of peace guards our hearts and minds. When peace rules in me, my heart and mind are protected from what the enemy would like to do in me. His lies roll off my back and I can stand in who I am. Make every effort to develop peace as a lifestyle. While some personality types may be more likely to worry, this is not a personality issue. It is an issue of choice. I choose to walk in peace. I choose to take time to get God's perspective on what I am facing. I choose to believe what He says rather than what the circumstances will tell me. Choosing peace for yourself will impact your classroom in a huge way. Use your own personal soaking times to establish the truth inside of you of who He is. Worship Him for His greatness, His goodness and His absolute love and devotion for you. When you have begun to establish peace in your own heart it is time to introduce your students to the concept of soaking and bringing peace to your classroom.

Before starting to introduce soaking to your students you may wish to discuss with the class what peace looks and feels like. Have them contrast peace versus anxiety or peace versus conflict. Ask them to choose which they would prefer to feel. Have them picture and describe things that bring them peace or represent peace to them.

For some that might be an image of soft white clouds. Others will picture peace as a soft blanket or favorite soft toy. The image they have doesn't matter so much as they have something in their mind that represents peace to them. When you start your soaking time this picture will give them something to focus on while they are inviting peace into the room.

Put quiet, soothing music on and ask them to position themselves where they won't be distracted by others. Have your students invite peace quietly into the room in whatever way seems best to you. Allow time for them to experience the shift in atmosphere as they let go of stress and draw on peace. Debrief afterwards discussing how it felt before you invited peace and after. Highlight how they changed the atmosphere by what they did. Let them know that they can use the same process in other settings. Start with short increments of time and build students ability slowly as they get used to the concept. Many students have never learned to simply be still and quiet. It takes training and practice to perfect this skill.

Students don't need to lie on the floor to soak. They can sit at their desks with their heads down or their eyes closed. Give them freedom to sit in a book corner or other appropriate space. How you manage the physical logistics of this process will depend on your space and the age of your students. A few minutes spent in managing the peace level in your class will more than make up for the time you 'lost' for teaching.

Find other ways to make students aware of the peace 'thermostat' in your room. Maybe you could make a thermometer that represents the level and move an arrow according to the atmosphere in your room. When it reaches a level that you and your class are unhappy with ask them for strategies on how to restore peace.

Ask students to describe things that show or bring peace. Have them write about or draw those images and display them in your classroom. Help them to recognize and deal with things that regularly try and steal their peace. Give time before tests or exams for students to draw on peace and dispel their anxiety.

Give time before tests or exams for students to draw on peace and dispel their anxiety.

Older students may need to understand why they are developing peace by researching the effect of stress on their ability to learn. Research on stress shows that it increases hormone levels that inhibit learning. Functions such as memory, reasoning, self-control and even impulse control are impacted by the release of stress hormones. (Edudemic; How Stress Affects the Brain During Learning) Give room for students to take a few moments to deal with their own lack of peace at the start of class by taking time to release stress and invite peace. Remember that God is the Prince of Peace and loves to show up whether your students know who He is or not. You own the atmosphere in the classroom and set the stage by Who you have already invited into your classroom.

QUESTIONS FOR ACTION

- What do I believe about the effect of peace on me and on my students?

- Do I believe that the Prince of Peace will show up if my students open themselves to peace?

- Do I believe that I have the ability to create an atmosphere of peace no matter what the students bring in to the atmosphere?

- What challenges my ability to carry peace?

- How does my peace positively affect the class?

- How does my lack of peace impact them?

- How does God want you to partner with Him as the Prince of Peace in your classroom?

- What does peace look like, feel like and sound like in a classroom?

- What does God want you to do this week to grow in peace in your life?

- What does God want you to do this week to grow your level of peace in the classroom?

DEALING WITH LIES
Developing Students Who Know the Truth about Themselves

JANINE MASON

Believing a lie can seriously ruin your day, and big people are not the only ones who struggle to believe the truth about themselves. Many times when we encounter a student who is having a bad day, it is because they are believing lies about themselves. We can, and should, tell them the truth, but next time they have a problem, they will need to come back to us or another adult they trust to access the truth again. The alternative is to teach them how to access the truth for themselves.

Many times when we encounter a student who is having a bad day, it is because they are believing lies about themselves.

Children are fed a multitude of lies by the world around them. Media tells them how they should look, the style of clothes to wear, and what brands they have to wear to be successful. Parents and teachers often set unrealistic expectations, and the enemy highlights to them everywhere that they don't feel they measure up. In the midst of all this noise, there is a voice of truth speaking. It is our job to help our students hear it.

My daughter Holly was seven when we first saw lies begin to impact her learning. She was in a combination class of first and second graders and was doing well with her spelling. Her teacher and I decided to increase the challenge by progressing her to a different, more challenging spelling list. At first she loved the challenge list and was responding well. After a few weeks, however, I started to notice her reluctance growing during spelling practice at home. It came to a head one day when I asked her to write down a few of the words she was having trouble with as I went to check the mailbox. I walked back into the house to find a tear-stained and angry seven-year-old thrusting the words she had written into my face and trying to exit "stage right" as fast as she could. I was confused. How did a child who was perfectly fine one minute turn into a defiant, crying child that fast? What had gone on while I was out of the room? The size of the reaction seemed out of proportion to the stimulus. It was time to talk.

The truth took some getting to. After chatting about it for a while, Holly finally blurted out, "I'm not smart. A first grader can spell a word that I can't spell." A few weeks before, Holly had noticed a girl in a lower grade spelling a word she couldn't spell. That was all it took for her to decide that she wasn't smart. The more she had believed the lie, the more resentful she had gotten. I told her that she was smart, but she wasn't buying it. It was time to teach her to find and fight for the truth about herself.

I asked her what she heard in her mind when she was having trouble spelling. "I'm not smart," was the reply. I wrote the lie on a piece of tissue and asked her to look at it. "Holly," I said, "what you are reading is a lie." We talked some more and flushed the tissue down the toilet together. I held her and instructed her to ask Jesus what the truth was. "He says I'm smart," she told me with a big grin. By the next day I had my happy speller back, and Holly has never struggled with spelling again.

During a separate season when she was struggling in another area, we went through a similar process. She flushed the lie, and I had her write the truth as a declaration. She placed the truth card at the end of her bed and said it out loud for several days until she had re-established it as the truth in her mind.

Our children are able to hear the truth from God at a young age. When we arm them with tools to access the truth, we arm them to become powerful overcomers in life.

The key is to teach the students that believing a lie destroys their life, but believing the truth brings freedom and joy.

One of our junior elementary classes did this together after the teacher had felt that several of the students were struggling with lies. She played worship music and instructed the students to ask the Lord to show them the lies they were believing about themselves. They then took the lies they were believing, "threw them to the ground," and stomped on them. It became a joyful "stomping party" as students got rid of the lies that had been plaguing them. She then gave the students time to ask the Lord the truth about themselves. One particularly attractive girl had been believing that she was ugly. She heard the Lord tell her how beautiful she was, and with a huge grin told everyone, "Now I know I am pretty again."

89

There are other ways to have the kids record the lies before you destroy them. You can write them on paper and burn them in a trash can, write them on balloons and pop them, use the tissue trick (harder with a whole class), or have a stomping party of your own. Whatever you do, the key is to teach the students that believing a lie destroys their life, but believing the truth brings freedom and joy. Having them destroy a physical representation of the lie is a powerful picture of what is going on inside of them. Reinforcing the truth using declarations is a great way to establish a new way of thinking.

SUMMARY

Developing Students Who Know the Truth about Themselves

The Bible says that you shall know the truth, and the truth shall set you free (John 8:32). Our students are under assault from lies presented through the media, from the people around them, and from the enemy of their souls. These influences are feeding them lies about themselves and the world around them in order to steal their joy and hope. Many students today struggle to find even one thing they like about themselves. It's no wonder that they struggle with a lack of hope.

Our classrooms can become a lie-free zone where we teach students to discover the truth and restore hope to their generation.

Our classrooms can become a lie-free zone where we teach students to discover the truth and restore hope to their generation. On the surface, this seems like an insurmountable task. How can we as educators, with a limited amount of time and input into a young person's life, stand against the overwhelming flood of negative thinking in his or her life? Without God, the task may seem too difficult, but with Him, there is a way. The first change that needs to happen is for you to believe that the Spirit of Truth (Jesus) is more powerful than the lies that are trying to recruit this generation. We as educators need to renew our thinking and align with a Heavenly perspective. His word says that "all things are possible for those who believe" (Mark 9:23). The question is this: will you step into belief and work with the Holy Spirit to bring students into truth?

KEY MINDSETS

- I partner with the Holy Spirit to bring truth to my students.

- I believe that God can bring truth into my classroom and set students free.

- God can show up as the Spirit of Truth and show students what is real.

- The way students see themselves (their beliefs) is the key to their learning.

MAKING IT REAL

Students need to know that what they believe impacts their learning more than anything else. If a student believes that he or she is a bad student and is incapable of succeeding in a certain subject, all your fancy teaching methods will fall on deaf ears until you can change the belief inside. Most teachers only deal with what a student believes as a side issue rather than tackling student beliefs as a critical theme to student success. Getting your students on board with the importance of beliefs is going to make the process of changing their thinking easier.

Most teachers only deal with what a student believes as a side issue rather than tackling student beliefs as a critical theme to student success.

With this in mind, set up some sort of demonstration that illustrates the power of beliefs. Use this to initiate a discussion around what we believe and its effects. When working with adults, we ask the class to respond honestly to a statement that we will put up on the overhead screen. We then put up a radical statement such as "Prisons will be obsolete in ten years." The students are then given an opportunity to discuss why they believe (and almost all do) that prisons cannot be obsolete in ten years' time. Once we have had a robust discussion of the "ridiculousness" of that statement, we talk about what the Bible says about it. The Bible says that nothing is impossible. We ask our audience to use that truth as a springboard to discuss how the statement could be made true. Suddenly creative ideas begin to flow as the class perspective changes and hope is allowed to rise. Finally we make the connection for our class that

93

the only thing that changed from one discussion to the next was that they changed what they believed. Creativity is released when we believe that something is possible. A belief that something can't change (or that I can't learn) stifles the will to even try.

Another tool I have used to demonstrate the power of beliefs is to have students take on a negative thought. With older students I will ask them to adopt, for a short time, the thought that they cannot cope and are overwhelmed. I ask them to roll the thought that they are overwhelmed in their mind for thirty seconds and pretend like they believe it. I ask them to be aware of what is happening in their bodies and emotions as they adopt that belief. Invariably I get the response that they could feel their bodies react, and the mood (atmosphere) of the class takes a nosedive. The great thing is that almost everyone can feel it both personally and corporately. You can then lead a discussion on how thinking negatively impacts the atmosphere even when you only adopt that thought for a few seconds. Be sure to have them then adopt a thought that is positive and that will restore hope to your students. Again, have them discuss what happens when they choose a good belief.

There's a scene in the movie *Indiana Jones and the Last Crusade* that demonstrates the power of what we believe beautifully. You can tell the story or show the movie clip with enough background for your students to understand what is happening. Indiana (the hero) is trying to save his father. Between Indy and the only thing that can heal his father is an impassable chasm. There is no way for him to use his trusty whip to swing across the gap, and all other paths have proved fruitless. It seems as though death is imminent, and Indiana can hear the cries of his dying father in the background. In short, the circumstances seem impossible. But then! Then Indiana realizes that the ancient writings in his hand say that there is a way across that will require a leap of faith. As he steps into the chasm, an invisible bridge appears underneath his feet, and all is made right with his world. The thing that saved Indiana and his father was that Indiana believed the truth. Without being armed with the truth, they would have perished.

After watching or listening to the story, I then ask the students to look at a wall in the classroom that has no door in it and tell them to imagine that all they ever wanted was behind that wall. They can only access it through that wall, not through any other means. I tell them if they just look at the wall and think there is no way through, then they won't try and find what they are looking for. But if I tell them that there is a way through, that it is just hidden from them, they will search until they find it.

Having good beliefs is like searching for the hidden way to all they ever wanted. Tell them that they can access success in schooling and in life if they are prepared to believe that there is a way through. Now you can begin to discuss what beliefs are holding them back. Even younger students can usually (with some help) articulate the negative things that they believe that stop them from learning, making friends, or thriving. Help them identify the wrong beliefs and then replace them with new ones. Make your classroom a negativity-free zone where you won't tolerate students partnering with unhealthy beliefs. Tell them the truth often and encourage them to help one another believe the best about themselves.

Make your classroom a negativity-free zone where you won't tolerate students partnering with unhealthy beliefs.

Once you have established that believing the truth is a key to success, discuss with your class how to find and establish good beliefs. As it becomes part of the culture to believe and speak well about themselves, the students will reinforce good behavior themselves.

I recently heard a story of how a kindergarten class did this with no teacher intervention. One little boy was verbally pulling himself down during a computer class, saying he couldn't do something. Several of his classmates immediately turned to him and told him, "That's not true. That's not who you are. Don't say that. We say the truth about ourselves in this class, and that's not true."

QUESTIONS FOR ACTION

- What do I believe that God can do in my class today to change the beliefs of students?

- What do I believe about my students?

- How does that belief show up in my teaching style?

- How is that reflected in how they behave? (both positively and negatively)

- In what areas do I believe lies about myself?

- How do the lies I believe show up in my language?

- What is this modeling to my students?

- What is the truth about who I am?

- What breakthroughs in thinking do I need to have in order to partner with God to bring truth?

- What strategies does God have for bringing truth into my classroom?

HONOR BOOT CAMP
Teaching Freedom and Responsibility

SARA RUST

Classroom management. For teachers who have a natural bent towards excellent leadership, order, and control in the classroom, I tip my hat. In my first years of teaching, it admittedly wasn't my strong suit. Like a new student driver with so many directions to be looking and things to be mindful of, during my first years of teaching, I found it challenging to keep on top of everything needing to be tended to. I didn't realize that teachers had slightly superhuman tendencies, especially when it comes to multitasking until I became one. At any given moment in a class, a teacher may be simultaneously processing:

That kid can't sit still. I need to address that.

That kid doesn't speak much English. I'll need to remember that.

That one keeps leaning back in their chair. I'll need to stop that.

That one now needs an ice pack for their elbow. I'll need to catch them up later.

The kids are looking bored. I'll need to liven things up to keep them engaged.

I've got two kids out with the flu. I'll need to get them their work and figure out when to reteach it to them.

I've gotta pee. I need to address that.

That kid looks upset and doesn't want to talk to his best bud. I may need to see what happened at recess.

This lesson is taking longer than expected. I'll have to re-plan this week's lesson plans to accommodate.

I forgot to pack my lunch. Maybe I should just work though it anyway.

Is the principal here to observe me?

Managing a class gets easier with practice. I always tell new teachers this—that it really is like driving a car, and as overwhelming as it can be in the beginning, things do become second nature after a while. After my second year of teaching, I went away for the summer and prayed about ways to improve my classroom management for the coming year. I found myself drawn to a familiar parable. In Matthew 25, Jesus describes a man who, before going on a journey, entrusts his property to his servants. When the master hears the report of good stewardship from some of his servants he responds, "Well done, good and faithful servant. You have been faithful over a little; I will set you over much. Enter into the joy of your master" (Matthew 25:21). I began to think about how to help my students understand how to take care of the things God has entrusted to them (school property, friends, assignments, etc.)

With Jesus' words twirling in my mind, I created a list of basic things I wanted my class to do well. These were items a teacher would commonly cover in their classroom management plan: how to walk in a line, how to clean up their tables, how to be ready to work when coming in from recess, and so on. I wrote the items on a large poster board like a checklist, and at the top I titled it

"Honor Boot Camp." I hung the poster on the classroom wall. I then bought yellow caution tape from the dollar store and taped off various items in the room, from our cozy reading area stuffed with pillows, to our worship flags, to our end of the week treasure box. Everything was ready for the first day of school.

"Well done, good and faithful servant. You have been faithful over a little; I will set you over much."

I greeted my students at the door, and we made our way inside. They took their seats, and we made our way through various orientation items. At last it was time to unveil the Honor Boot Camp.

"Does anyone notice the yellow tape?" I asked. Little heads nodded and replied.

"Yes, can we use the reading area?" one hopeful student asked.

"Not yet, but you can earn your reading area back. Does anyone see the poster board on the wall? What does it say?"

As I drew their attention to the Honor Boot Camp poster, I shared that this year, they would need to earn the use of the reading area, the worship fabrics, the treasure box, trips to our prayer house, etc. by showing honor to me, to each other, and to our school. As they began to learn how to do the things on the list as a class, I would tear off the tape.

I shared with them the parable of the talents from Matthew 25. I reiterated that when they were faithful with a little, I would entrust them with more. I set different parameters for items on the list. Sometimes there was an actual number; for example, "I need to see

20 perfect lines" or "I need to see you handle transitioning to PE well this week" based on how much practice I felt they would need for these things to become habit. The students were ready, excited, and motivated. They began to manage themselves without much of my help, and week by week, the tape came down.

Honor Boot Camp was so effective for my class, the teacher next door began implementing it in her class. Throughout the year the poster remained on the wall, and if needed, I could "reset" the class by sending us back to boot camp to check things off the list again.

What I loved most about this tool for classroom management was that it created opportunities to talk with the class about working as a team, stewardship, and what it practically means to walk in honor. As I've continued to grow as a teacher and in classroom management, I still find God's Word a wonder for uncovering new strategies.

SUMMARY
Teaching Freedom and Responsibility

Many teachers are looking for the holy grail of classroom management—a way to control the students that parade through their classrooms year after year. Different tools are added to their tool belt as they learn strategies to corral the most difficult of students through a variety of methods. Sara's Honor Boot Camp is another such tool to add to your tool belt, although I suspect that many of you already use the strategy of withholding certain privileges until they are "earned" in your classroom.

What made this tool stand out to me is that the heart of it and the application of it were different than what's experienced in many classrooms. Sara didn't just rope off the "cool" stuff in the classroom and tell students they had to earn it by making the right choices. She taught them a Kingdom Principle that will set the students up for life. She used the story from Matthew 25 to teach students that if you are faithful with little, you can be entrusted with much. Whether students hear that principle straight from scripture or through another avenue, the Kingdom principle will play out in their lives whether they like it or not. Allowing students to learn the principle of stewardship or faithfulness in the context of their behavior allows them to take ownership of their behavior to a whole new level. No longer is it about you needing to control their outward behavior; it now becomes about them internally managing themselves (becoming responsible) in order to access greater freedom.

KEY MINDSETS

- Freedom and responsibility go hand in hand.

- If I am faithful over little, then I will be entrusted with much.

- My goal is to teach self-management rather than exert external control.

- I teach students truths that set them up for success.

- I manage my class through teaching self-control rather than through fear.

MAKING IT REAL

Bethel Christian School uses a variety of behavior management strategies and tools. These are predominantly sourced from *Loving Our Kids on Purpose* (Danny Silk) and *Capturing Kids' Hearts* (curriculum from the Flippen Group). Both these sources have at their heart the idea that classroom management should be relationally based rather than fear based. Controlling the classroom becomes less about controlling the students through fear of punishment and more about teaching them self-management.

Controlling the classroom becomes less about controlling the students through fear of punishment and more about teaching them self-management.

On the surface, the strategies can look similar. Sara's roping off the reading corner at the start of the school year could look like a hardhearted challenge to "behave or else you miss out." It wasn't. Instead it was a loving invitation to students to grow in their ability to manage themselves (show faithfulness) so she could release more freedom to them. Sara laid out very clearly her goal of helping them learn to look after the things they had been given so that they could access more. In her case, she was able to teach directly from the Bible to train students in the principle of faithfulness. By putting the Honor Boot Camp in the context of learning the principle, she not only taught students how she expected them to behave but she also clearly taught them and allowed them to experience earning freedom through responsibility.

The underlying value that shows up in all the behavior management strategies that we at Bethel Christian School seek to employ is that *you are responsible for you*. As a student, we will clearly communicate what we need from you, discuss that with you, and you then get to choose your way into more or less freedom. The language is very much designed to let students know that they are responsible for themselves. Interactions with individual students or whole classes will use language that reminds students that they are not powerless in this equation. They have an opportunity to show teachers that they know how to manage themselves really well and thus earn more and more freedom. Or conversely, they get to show that they choose not to follow through with what is expected and therefore cannot be trusted with more responsibility.

You are responsible for you.

Younger students need you to help them understand that this is not something that happens to them because they are young. They tend to think that one day they will grow up and be old enough to ignore the expectations of others. Teach these students that adults are still working through the same process. When I work hard for an employer and show that I can fulfill his or her expectations and that I manage myself without their input, I am likely to get promoted. When I show that I can manage myself well and take responsibility for myself in my relational world, I grow my friendships.

Students typically don't think about how the things you are teaching them show up in real life. Don't turn it into a lecture, just use every opportunity to reinforce the principle. Where does this show up in the stories they are reading? How do the characters in those books show this principle? Who in the world of science or history demonstrates this well? Show them how it connects in the world of sports teams and drama clubs. Those that can be trusted to attend practices tend to get to do more. There are opportunities everywhere to teach students that they are not victims, but that they have the power to influence how much freedom they get.

Be aware of your own language and what it communicates to students. They are watching to see if you believe what you say. Does your language indicate that you are able to manage yourself? Does it say that you believe that they can make good choices? You have a wonderful opportunity to teach them that their success in life is primarily determined by how well they manage themselves.

You have a wonderful opportunity to teach them that
their success in life is primarily determined by
how well they manage themselves.

The challenge to implementing this kind of behavior management strategy is that it forces us to change the way we think and interact with students. Love and honor must become the foundation of how we interact with them rather than fear and control. This is a hard transition for many who have been trained all their lives in tools that use fear as the foundation of controlling a class. You will need to face your own beliefs and change your heart attitudes in order to fully empower your students to make their choices. You can find out more about this radical approach by reading *Loving Our Kids on Purpose* by Danny Silk.

QUESTIONS FOR ACTION

- Is my behavior management style marked by fear of consequences or by love?

- In what ways can I lead from love versus fear?

- How can I empower students to take ownership of their behavior?

- What stops me from setting good boundaries and following through?

- What do I think setting firm boundaries says about me?

- What internal beliefs need to change for me to enforce boundaries?

- How do I keep the long-term goal in focus while dealing with the day-to-day challenges?

- Is my need to be liked as a teacher sabotaging my classroom management?

- How does my own experience as a child impact on my classroom management?

- What skills can I teach my students that bring internal rather than external control?

I HAVE A DREAM
The Art of Keeping Hope Alive

JANINE MASON

I have a dream. I dream that we will teach the world to have radical hope again. I have a dream that young people everywhere (and those not so young) will see the dreams and desires of their heart and will know that they were put on the earth to fulfill them. I have a dream that every young person exiting school will leave with a sense of purpose and will know how he or she is uniquely made to live out that purpose. I have a dream that this new sense of hope and purpose will create an atmosphere where cures for diseases will be found, where life-giving innovations will be released, and joy will be unleashed upon the earth. Simply put, I have a dream that people will learn to dream again.

Children are natural dreamers. The wonderful thing about working with the very young is that they have not yet been taught what is impossible. Kindergartners are not generally caught up in the technicalities of how to make their dream come true. They just believe that they can be a superhero, the president, or someone famous. Their life experience has not yet taught them what is "impossible." We look on and write off their innate faith as childish foolishness. We fail to realize that it is this very substance, their faith, that is the reason that God tells us to become like little children. I have become convinced that one of our jobs as Kingdom educators is to keep the belief that "nothing is impossible" alive in our students' hearts. One of the areas wherein we can do this is the area of dreams.

I have become convinced that one of our jobs as Kingdom educators is to keep the belief that "nothing is impossible" alive in our students' hearts.

We believe that dreamers are carriers of hope. We believe that students who know their dreams and believe that they are possible, carry a hope that is unstoppable. Because of this, we have begun to teach our students to pay attention to their dreams. No, we don't have sleeping in class. We're not talking about the dreams they have at night. We are talking about the dreams that God placed in their hearts that reveal the way they are made to impact the world.

Dreaming shows up in a number of ways throughout our school, finding different expressions at different ages. Our third and fourth graders, at a certain stage of the year, have an opportunity to do a multifaceted project on "What makes me come alive." During that module, students will do research on the area that they are passionate about, answer questions and write about different aspects of their dream, and ultimately do a verbal presentation to the class. This presentation can include singing, dancing, or showing the class an object that they have created that relates to their dream. Students are encouraged to embrace and express their individuality and to think about how they might move towards their dream. As they work through the project, not only are they learning tools that they can use throughout their lives to move towards other dreams, but they are also having someone speak approval and blessing over their dream. That a teacher would show interest and pay attention to what is important to them makes a powerful statement to students.

Students are encouraged to embrace and express their individuality and to think about how they might move towards their dream.

At the top end of the school, seventh and eighth graders are exposed to the concept of dreaming and pursuing their dreams through a bi-weekly dream class. Here they are encouraged to discover and record the things that they are passionate about. Each is given a dream journal where they record not only the dreams that they have but also the process of moving towards those dreams. Throughout the class, the teacher pours encouragement on them and teaches them that nothing is impossible. She also gives them practical keys in moving towards their dreams, and the students are encouraged to take steps towards making their dreams a reality. Teachers keep it real by sharing their own experiences and by talking about dealing with disappointment and how to keep motivation alive.

Dreaming is also intentionally becoming a part of our culture by becoming part of the language of the school. Other teachers will set assignments that give students opportunities to express their dreams, and there is an atmosphere of hope and possibility that pervades the school.

Teaching students to dream will cost you something. You will have to face your own sense of disappointment in the areas where you have not seen what you wanted or expected. At times you will see students that you think are dreaming of impossible things, and you will want to protect them from the disappointment you think is surely coming. You will have a choice of protecting them from being disappointed or supporting them through it and teaching them to still keep reaching for the stars.

Teaching students to dream will cost you something.

A few years ago, I came across a quote that keeps my thinking straight in this area.

"Never tell a young person that something can't be done. God may have been waiting centuries for someone ignorant of the impossible to do that very thing." G.M. Trevelyan (English historian, 1876-1962)

The child in your class that is dreaming of discovering and colonizing a new planet (like one of our students was) may be the next space traveller who will do just that. Don't discount a student's dream because it looks scary to you. Use questions to get to the heart of it and ask God what He has to say about it. It may be that you see before you the student who has the potential to bring the next big breakthrough to the world. The question is, will you be the teacher that supports them in it or a teacher that causes them to give up before they even start?

SUMMARY
The Art of Keeping Hope Alive

[12] "Hope deferred makes the heart sick,
but when the desire comes, it is a tree of life."

Proverbs 13:12

God places dreams and desires inside of us that He longs for us to fulfill. Our dreams are an indication of who we are made to be and what we are to contribute to planet earth.

Our dreams are an indication of who we are made to be and what we are to contribute to planet earth.

God is a good Father that wants the best for His children. It is a cruel parent that would give a brand-new shiny bike to a child and then tell the child that they could not ride it. Neither does God give us dreams that He won't also help us to fulfill in some way. Teaching students to dream and to believe for the impossible is the thing that keeps hope alive. We must deal with our own beliefs about dreaming in order to model and teach about the power of living our dreams.

KEY MINDSETS

- Dreaming is vital to students thriving.

- God has the ability to deal with wrong motives for dreams.

- With God, nothing is impossible.

- Desires of the heart are given by God and show who we were made to be.

- God wants to fulfill the heart of every dream.

- Failure isn't fatal; it's a normal part of growth.

- Disappointment cripples my ability to dream if I don't deal with it.

- I will not let the voice of disappointment speak louder than the truth.

MAKING IT REAL

As a Director of Dream Culture, I have been working with leaders of organizations for a number of years now, and the first question that many will ask is, "What is the best thing I can do to get my people dreaming?" As a teacher you may be asking the same question. My answer will be the same to you as to a pastor or CEO of an organization. If you want to get your people (students) to dream, the best thing you can do is to live your dreams yourself and to let them in on the process. Your students are watching what you do more than you realize, and what you are living speaks more to them than what you are saying.

So what can it look like to create a culture where hope is abundant and following your dreams is normal? I think it has three parts. The first is genuinely following your own dreams and sharing your journey with your students. Dreams don't have to be huge, world-changing dreams to be impactful. Sharing with your students that you have always wanted to take a cooking class or have a part in the local theater shows them that it is normal to have and pursue dreams. When you share the joy of a dream fulfilled, it can't help but inspire students to pursue their own dreams.

Don't be afraid, though, to share the speed bumps along the way. The leader of our dream class for our seventh and eighth graders called a meeting with me to ask what she should do. "I shared with all the classes how I had applied for a college course, and I didn't get in," she said. "I don't know what to tell them. I don't want them to feel let down." I encouraged her to share with her students what she was feeling and how she was going to move forward. It was a perfect learning experience. The students got an up-close view of how to walk through disappointment and how to keep going when it doesn't work out the first time.

The second part is to show a genuine interest in the dreams of your students. As you build relationships with them, ask what interests they have and look for the areas they are passionate about. Make talking about dreams a normal part of life. Ask questions about and celebrate progress. Commiserate about any setbacks and encourage them to get back up and try again. You may be the only adult who is providing encouragement to pursue that dream. For many educators, the desire to turn the dream into something we know they can accomplish is greater than our desire to champion them in their pursuit. A student who has had encouragement poured on them and who fails in an attempt to attain a dream is actually more likely to do something significant in the world than one who has had their dreams squashed and never attempted anything.

Make talking about dreams a normal part of life.

The thing that often stops us cheering our students on is our concern that they might not make it. We decide that what they are dreaming of seems impossible. That makes us nervous, so we ask them to make the dream smaller so we feel better about their chances of "making it." I wonder if the Wright brothers dreamed of flying while at school. I wonder what their teachers would have said if they had shared their dream. There was a time when space exploration was nothing but a dream. I wonder what teachers in that era told their students about their dreams to be in space. What are the new frontiers that face the students of today? Who are we to try to rescue our students from those dreams?

But what about the scrawny student who wants to be a defensive lineman or the student with the low IQ who wants to be a doctor? Shouldn't we let them know that their dream is impossible to save them some heartache? Let me propose a different line of attack.

114

Instead of being the one who reduces their dreams and teaches them to approach life this way, how about you become their biggest champion instead. From that place of cheering them on, begin to ask them questions. Help them to uncover the reason they want to be a lineman on the local team or a doctor. Ask them questions about what it takes to live that dream. Help them research the path to the dream. Many will work out all on their own that their dream is not "realistic," but in the process they will uncover what is really important. A dream to be a doctor may really be a dream to always have enough money, and there are many roads to that dream. A dream to be a lineman may be a dream to feel significant, and that can be achieved in many ways. Your goal is to pour encouragement on your students so you're coming from a place of trust when you discuss the decisions they are making.

Look for ways to incorporate dreaming within your curriculum.

The third thing you can do to create a culture where dreaming flourishes is to look for ways to incorporate dreaming within your curriculum. This means that students have an opportunity to explore what they are most passionate about within the confines of school. It also gives a clear message that pursuing your dream is an important part of life. Set essays around dream topics such as, "What makes you come alive?" or "How I want to change the world." Teach students how to research by letting them research a topic associated with their dream. Free reading assignments can be set to encourage students to read about heroes that are living a dream similar to theirs. There are countless ways to bring the topic of dreaming into your curriculum.

The one area that stops most of us from dreaming and encouraging others to dream is disappointment. As adults, most of us have had a broken dream or two, and we have had to deal with the pain of loss. We know how painful it is to have the thrill of high expectations only to have them dashed when something didn't work out how we thought. Because we have experienced this, sometimes over and over again, we want to save the young people in our lives from the same pain. Everything inside of you is wired to protect your charges from harm. It is hard at times to turn the voice of past disappointment down in order to train your students to dream.

As a mother, I have had the opportunity to walk this out with my own children.

Hannah, my eldest, had a dream to have a significant role in one of the school dramas. In sixth grade she had a role with six lines, and by seventh grade she was anticipating promotion. The day of the auditions came, and Hannah felt she had done quite well. She chatted on and on about the role that she most wanted and hoped she'd get. Everything inside of me wanted to prepare her for the possibility that she might not get the part she wanted. I didn't want her to get hurt. At the same time, I wanted her to believe for the best and trust that nothing is impossible. So every time the conversation turned to the play, I simply encouraged her to believe that God's best for her would happen.

The day the cast list was released came, and I drove to pick the kids up from school. I didn't have to ask how it went; I could see from the tear-stained face that all was not well. By the time we got home, she could speak enough to say she had a part with one line. Just one line. She was devastated, and my heart was crushed on her behalf. She cried and cried and then cried some more. She was ready to quit the whole drama thing. "I never want to do this again. What's the point if I do my best and all I can get is a part with one line? How am I going to make it through all those rehearsals when my friends will be doing lots of speaking and I'll be feeling like a loser?" That evening, hours later, I popped my head around the corner of her room. "Are you doing okay?" I asked. "I may never be okay again," was her reply. Oh my aching mother's heart!

It was a painful day for all of us. But slowly, after I had comforted and listened, and listened and comforted, I could begin to talk to Hannah about the future. We arranged to meet the drama teacher the next day. She was able to explain far better than I could why Hannah didn't get the part and what she could do to grow. She encouraged her to keep a great attitude, to apply herself to the understudy role she had been given, and to be at every practice. She left that meeting with fresh hope and confidence and new insight into what goes in to casting people for school dramas. By the time that the drama actually happened, Hannah had a number of extra lines. Her diligence and good attitude had paid off, and she was rewarded with increase. Hannah learned some invaluable lessons that day that have set her up for life. I could have saved her the pain of that horrible day, but in doing so, I would have had to break that precious part inside of her that is wired to see that nothing is impossible. Instead I let her feel the pain of disappointment and gave her faith to believe that tomorrow is a new day. At the time of writing, Hannah is preparing for her role in this year's school drama. It is not the lead, but it has all the components of the role that she dreamed of.

Our students are going to experience disappointment along the way. There are times when God won't show up in the way they expected. As important adults in their lives, we are trained to protect them from imminent danger, but let us be wise and not teach them to lower their expectations to only what is possible. Instead let us cry with them and teach them to deal with disappointment with renewed faith for the days that are ahead. Let us be a generation of educators and parents that protect the "nothing is impossible" part of our children, determined to keep it alive and learn from it ourselves.

Every day in your classroom, your students share their lives with you. You see both their triumphs and their tragedies, at least the ones that play out in your classroom. How you respond to those moments goes a long way in shaping what those moments mean in the larger context of life. Your response to a "failure" shows a student whether failure is fatal or a normal part of growth. The way you speak about those things that look and seem impossible to a student trains them to either constantly stretch to believe for more, or to shut down and reduce their expectation.

QUESTIONS FOR ACTION

- How has your desire to protect students from disappointment affected your ability to encourage them to dream big?

- What will you do differently in the future?

- What do you believe about dreams? What mindsets stop you pursuing your own dreams? What mindsets does God want to change?

- How has disappointment affected your own ability to dream? What does God say about that?

- What dreams does God want to reignite in you?

- How can you set up a culture of pursuing dreams within your classroom?

- What is the first step in doing this?

- Where could dreams show up in your curriculum?

10

BLESSING OUR BODIES AND OUR BRAINS
The Power of Declaration

LINDSAY BROWN

Education is an ever-changing beauty. New curriculums, pedagogy, class sizes, standardized testing, etc. are in constant flux. One thing remains the same: teachers and their love for what they do, no matter what the new trend. We educate because there will always be a child ready to learn, a classroom ready to explode with new adventures.

Just like the education pendulum is always swinging, our teaching tools are constantly changing. In my time teaching, I have seen soaring successes and fabulous failures. The most effective tools I have in my teacher tool belt are the ones that came out of moments of sweet inspiration and complete frustration.

In my experience, children are the most confident human beings, particularly kindergarten-age children. They take risks that most adults would tremble to even imagine, and yet every risk is a success, whether it was a triumph or not. Children are created to be bold, daring, and secure in who they are, no matter what the circumstance. But so often, even at the most innocent of ages, I hear children say, "I can't" or "I'm not good at this" or "I can't try that." Early in my kindergarten career, I began to ask myself, where and when did these confident children take on these significant insecurities?

Children are created to be bold, daring, and secure in who they are, no matter what the circumstance.

I can still remember the moment I learned how to read. It was positively magical. I can also remember the moment I began to dislike math. Actually, detest would be a better description of my feelings toward math as a child and a young adult. The moment I was "demoted" to the lower math class in third grade changed the landscape of my experience with anything math related. Every struggle and bad grade confirmed my insecurity. I would often say, "I'm so bad at math." All of my experiences were confirmation and reiterated the great divide in my heart between my strengths and my obvious weakness.

I can't imagine a world where I could let my experience dictate how my students would experience learning. Childhood is too short to be stuck in insecurities. It saddens my heart when I hear such little ones declare, "I can't read," or "I don't know, I'm not that good at math," or "I'm stupid." These are surprisingly common in my confident kindergarteners.

I have been on a journey, learning the impact words have and the truths they can create in our unsuspecting minds. We were created to believe in ourselves. Part of my journey has been discovering the power of my words.

On one particular day in my classroom, my students and I were finishing our calendar time, and I heard the sweetest whisper from the Holy Spirit, "You are learning to make positive declarations; teach your students the same."

I had my students all stand up, and I began to make declarations, inviting my kindergarteners to do the same. This is what we declared: "Brain, you are amazing. You think well. Do your job today. Eyes, you see clearly. You are amazing. Do your job today. Ears, you are good listeners. Listen well today. Lips, you are amazing. Speak kind words today. Heart, you are amazing. Thanks for keeping me alive. Do your job today. Immune system, you are amazing. Thanks for keeping me healthy. Do your job today. Neighbor (the students look to someone next to them), you are fabulous. I see gold in you. Will you look for the gold in me today?!" At first my students thought I was the silliest teacher ever, but this moment was significant and transformative. Every day now in my class, we bless our bodies and our friends. Every day is another opportunity to create a new way of thinking in our brains and a new way of engaging with how we were created to believe in ourselves.

Every day is another opportunity to create a new way of thinking in our brains.

I knew I was onto something big a few weeks into our declarations. A father came to me and recounted a moment he had with his son playing checkers. He said his son was struggling in the game and he said to his dad, "I need a minute." My student turned around and began to say to himself. "OK brain, you can do this. You are a good brain. Do your job." The dad was surprised that his son was speaking to his brain. He said in a moment when his son would usually have given up, his pep talk to his brain kept him in the game. Instead of building a case for failure, my student chose to take control of any negative thoughts. He chose to believe he could and declared triumph over failure.

I am realizing no matter how old we are,

our beliefs dictate our success.

I am realizing no matter how old we are, our beliefs dictate our success. In my class before we start a new math activity, I will lead my students to declare over our brains, "Brain, you are amazing. You were created for math. Do your job today." Usually after we've had our lesson, we bless our brains again: "Brain, you did a great job! Keep up the great work." We do the same thing when we are about to read and after we read. "Brain, you were created to read. Do your job today." Giving our students the language to believe in themselves is a crucial element to their overall success.

SUMMARY
The Power of Declaration

Lindsay has taken the power of declaration and has harnessed it with her kindergartners to speak directly over their bodies and minds. She is training her class to see the different parts of their bodies and their mind as designed by God to do the things that are required of them at school and beyond. What I love about this tool is that she is teaching students at the start of their education to *see* themselves differently. She is directly coming against any mindset that her students' brains "can't do it" by reinforcing that they were made to learn and be successful. Proverbs 23:7 says that the way a man (or a student) thinks about himself will determine who he is. It is important that we teach our students that they were designed to learn.

KEY MINDSETS

- I use my tongue to speak life everywhere I go.

- My words have power to change how students see themselves.

- I teach students to see themselves as successful.

- God designed our bodies and brains to function at a high level.

- I choose to take control over all negative thoughts. I declare triumph over failure.

MAKING IT REAL

I remember when I first got my driver's license. There was a new sense of freedom as I drove myself where I wanted to go without having to consult with others. One particular day I was driving down a country road, and my attention wandered for a moment to the fields. When I turned my eyes back to the road, I realized the car in front had come to a stop, and I was almost up his tailpipe. The thought flitted through my shocked mind, "Every time I get behind the wheel, I hold the power of life and death in my hands. Wow, that's quite a responsibility." Quick as a flash, I heard the Lord say, "Every time you speak, you hold the same power in your tongue." Proverbs 18:21 says, "The power of life and death is in the tongue." Each day we get to decide how we will use our tongues. We can use them to sow life or destruction as we interact with our students. Not only do we get to sow life by the words we speak, but we also have the opportunity to train them to speak life over themselves as well.

So many of our students are exposed to influences that are toxic to their identities in the environment they live in. Even well-meaning parents speak careless words that attack the beliefs children have about themselves and their learning ability. Students learn from a young age to compare themselves with their peers, and unfortunately, many of the comparisons are at their expense. A student comes to your classroom, therefore, with a multitude of beliefs in place that are counterproductive to a learning environment. If we are to teach our students to a high level of success, we must train them to see themselves correctly and to speak the truth over themselves.

Psalm 139:13–14 For you formed my inward parts; You covered me in my mother's womb. I will praise You, for I am fearfully and wonderfully made, Marvelous are Your works, And that my soul knows very well.

The above Bible verses talk about how wonderfully God made the human body and mind. Have you stopped lately to think about how phenomenal it is? I mean seriously, God created a human body, mind, and spirit to interconnect and function in a way that scientists are only just beginning to understand. When we help our students realize that they have been put together in such an amazing way and that their brains are designed to learn, their ears to listen, and their eyes to see, they will have a different way of seeing themselves. We can help their focus shift from all the things they feel inadequate about and turn their attention to how well they were designed.

If we are to teach our students to a high level of success, we must train them to see themselves correctly and to speak the truth over themselves.

By making declarations over the different aspects of the students, Lindsay is helping them identify what needs to be functioning in order to do well her in her classroom. Lindsay's students are young. They love to make declarations over their eyes and ears and brains. The declarations help them to understand that their eyes, ears, and brains all need to be engaged with the lesson for them to be successful. Her declarations allow students to realize that their bodies were made to learn. It teaches her students that they can manage their bodies and work with them to be successful learners. Lindsay has taught them well and created a culture where it is normal to speak over our bodies to bring them into order. She also gives them opportunities to show leadership of this by allowing some students to lead the class in their declaration times.

So how could this look in your classroom? With younger students in any setting, you could train students in exactly the same way Lindsay does. Lead your students through the declarations below, adapt them to your class, or write your own.

Brain, you are amazing. You think well. Do your job today.

Eyes, you see clearly. You are amazing. Do your job today.

Ears, you are good listeners. Listen well today.

Lips, you are amazing. Speak kind words today.

Heart, you are amazing. Thanks for keeping me alive. Do your job today.

Immune system, you are amazing. Thanks for keeping me healthy. Do your job today.

The important thing is to create a culture where there is an understanding that every student has the capacity to learn well. Your goal is to teach your students that they are designed to learn and to reinforce this mindset with declarations and language within your classroom.

For older students, this may look like leading the class in realizing that our words have power and then asking them to harness that power in a constructive way. Find stories of successful people who have used the power of declarations in their journeys and use them to inspire your students.

As an example, I recently came across the story of Russell Redenbaugh. Redenbaugh lost his sight at 16 in a rocket-making venture gone wrong. Previously only an average student, he overcame poverty and his physical limitations to graduate fifth in his class at the prestigious Wharton Business School at the University of Pennsylvania. His many achievements include managing a $6 billion investment firm, sitting as a U.S. Civil Rights Commissioner and becoming a jiu-jitsu world champion three times. Redenbaugh attributes some of his success to the power of declaration. In fact he shares how, on the day he was told he would remain blind, he declared, "I will not be dependent, I will not be poor, I will not live at home. I will live in the world of the sighted doing sighted things." Redenbaugh says that the discovery of declarations is one of the most powerful things in all his years. "Declarations precede leaps and precipitate action," explains Redenbaugh. (http://www. shiftthenarrative.com/)

Once you have buy-in from your older students on the power of declarations, have them design declarations that you as a class want to speak over yourselves. Have them formulate declarations that are positive in nature rather than negative. It is better to declare "I am a hard worker" than to declare "I am not a slacker." Use your declarations to build a culture in your classroom that accentuates the positives and minimizes the negative. Use declarations to reinforce that every student can be successful.

QUESTIONS FOR ACTION

- Do I believe that my words have power in them?

- Do I believe that my students can change their life through declaration?

- What declarations do I need to speak over my life for breakthrough?

- What declarations does my class need?

- What benefits have I seen in my life when I use declarations?

- What is God declaring over me that I can agree with?

BEYOND THE CURRICULUM
Academics as a Vehicle for the Kingdom

TAWNY NOVOSAD

Teachers are lifelong learners. They are built, equipped, and hand-crafted to not only love and care for their pupils but also to instill in all of them the love of learning. How delightful is it that we can partner with the creator of the universe to instill something in our students that is far beyond our curriculum?

I'm going to paint a picture for you that I believe we, as teachers, can all relate to. After a particularly challenging week teaching a class of 23 first and second graders, it was FINALLY Friday! We were going to have a spelling test, do a fun science activity, and pretty much just enjoy and relax that day—so relaxed that I even dressed for the occasion with tennis shoes and an outfit that looked more appropriate for a gym than a classroom. This of course was the same morning that right before said spelling test, my assistant principal, Mrs. Armstrong, walks in for my first (and surprise) observation. I'm pretty sure all the blood ran down into my suddenly not-so-comfortable running shoes. Was my classroom heater suddenly kicking on? I whispered under my breath, "Holy Spirit, my lesson plans don't look so great for today; I'm dressed like I'm headed out for a jog, and I'm about to be observed by someone I

129

really respect. Can you just take over for me?" I heard the Holy Spirit reply with, "Trust me and don't veer from your plans." So, I didn't. I gave a spelling test and did the not hugely academic science lab, and the kids had fun. When I got my observation sheet returned to me, the vice principal had LOVED the lessons! She had written something in it that I had never even thought about. Something that I had always longed to do in a public school, but thought I was only allowed to do in a Christian school: I incorporated God into just about everything we covered.

Let me explain. For eight years I had taught, carefully veering around the most important thing in my life. I had to shake my head when I couldn't tell students the source of why these things occur in science or who to look to when their families were falling apart and they needed the Father's embrace. At Bethel Christian School, I felt as if I had finally been set free to release everything God had put in my spirit to give children for the past decade. So, I did it in every way I could. When Mrs. Armstrong observed my spelling test, the one I considered a complete bore to watch, she saw how I used Bible verses and declarations with spelling words in a sentence. When we did our science lab on electricity, she witnessed how excited I became when the kids and I could talk about the source of all of our light and how God created such amazing things as electricity.

I didn't realize this was a strength the Holy Spirit had given me until a special administrator pulled out the gold in me and recognized it as a gift.

I didn't realize this was a strength the Holy Spirit had given me until a special administrator pulled out the gold in me and recognized it as a gift. It encouraged me to not only keep doing it but to also find ways to tap into heaven in even the most mundane of academic necessities.

It shouldn't have been surprising that my boss found favor in what I did, because it wasn't me. When the Holy Spirit is right there whispering in our willing and listening ears, we are moved by His presence to create wonderful classroom scenarios. With a willing spirit, the Holy Spirit can create the most beautiful workmanship out of our lesson plans, activities, assignments, group tasks, and even our most menial work.

Lamentations 4:2 describes how the children of Zion are "valuable as fine gold" and says they are "regarded as clay pots, the work of the hands of the potter." These priceless students are worth so much more than all the gold in the world, yet they are pots of clay. We, as teachers, get to tag along with the Holy Spirit while He's molding, bending, sharpening, and fashioning them into the people He's designed them to be.

We, as teachers, get to tag along with the Holy Spirit while He's molding, bending, sharpening, and fashioning them into the people He's designed them to be.

Working with the Holy Spirit to mold our students and teach them the ways of the Kingdom can be challenging. I have found when I am personally challenged in this area, it has everything to do with where I am in my relationship with God. When I am feeling spiritually, emotionally, or physically drained and exhausted, I rely on my own strengths and capabilities too well. My goal becomes, let's just say it, to *survive* the day. When we are in that place we muddle through plans with hopes that no one throws a tantrum, throws up, or sees that you're hanging by a very thin, frail thread. These are the days that we especially need to hear Jesus championing us. When you feel like you can't take another step or do another thing, turn your ear to Him and listen for instructions. He wants to take you and your class well beyond just survival.

At the beginning of this past year, I was given a prophetic word that I was supposed to walk into my classroom every day and declare, "I am a GREAT teacher and the Holy Spirit is going to do AMAZING things in here!" It sounded a little silly at first, but I decided that if I teach my students to make declarations, I could make them too. I began doing this, and the Holy Spirit showed up! I asked for more! I wanted angelic visitations, and they came! I asked the Holy Spirit to give me more peace and patience than I had ever had with certain students, and He did! I asked for my students to have academic breakthroughs like never before, and they have!!! Thank you Jesus!

Your curriculum can become the greatest vehicle to teaching the Kingdom in your classroom if you will let it.

I challenge you to use your curriculum to teach Biblical principles and ask the Holy Spirit for creative ways to do this. Every book you read to your class can become a tool against the enemy, empowering your students with knowledge and understanding. The more your students are able to think, create, and imagine, the less they will fall victim to outsiders and the devil telling them they can't. Use every science lesson to display the works of His hands, every spelling test to teach and reinforce Kingdom principles. Your curriculum can become the greatest vehicle to teaching the Kingdom in your classroom if you will let it.

My prayer for you is that God will implement creative ways to meet academic needs that have never been done before. That He will release ways for you to cross bridges educationally that no one has ever crossed. I pray the Holy Spirit brings more academic breakthroughs in your classroom than anyone has ever seen. You will be known as the teacher where the "unteachable" students become overcomers and leaders in their class. Father I ask you to bring a new generation of thinkers, processors, and world changers that know you, love you, and want to share your love with the world.

"Education is the most powerful weapon which
you can use to change the world."

Nelson Mandela

SUMMARY

Academics as a Vehicle for the Kingdom

Many of us have felt boxed in by the restrictions of regulations or curriculum placed on us by our administration. We have come to believe, at least to some extent, that we are extremely limited in what we can teach about the Kingdom of God in our classrooms. Yet our students are wired by God for truth and are crying out to know what is real. Although we may not be able to mention the name of Jesus in some settings, we are able to teach His principles and His ways as we interact with our students. In many ways, who you are as a teacher is far more impacting to your students than the knowledge you carry and impart. Obviously we want to be highly skilled and competent in our teaching, but the impact you have beyond those skills and knowledge is what has the potential to shape your students for the rest of their lives and perhaps for eternity.

Every moment of the day, you are teaching your students something. Much of what they are learning and absorbing is not in the curriculum.

The reality is that every moment of the day, you are teaching your students something. Much of what they are learning and absorbing is not in the curriculum. It comes through observing the adults in their lives, namely you. You have the power to teach your students how to respond to conflict in your interactions with them. You have the power to train your students how to deal with stress as they watch you live it out before them. Does this then demand perfection from you in order to be a great teacher? No. It is simply

134

an invitation to recognize that every day holds a multitude of opportunities to interact with students, to be the Kingdom, and to thread an understanding of the Kingdom of God through every aspect of your curriculum.

KEY MINDSETS

- My curriculum is a vehicle to teach about the Kingdom.

- I am always teaching something.

- There are endless possibilities for teaching His ways in my classroom.

- God is bigger than any box I may put myself in.

- God has given me everything I need to live the Kingdom in my classroom.

MAKING IT REAL

Tawny is a master at integrating Kingdom values and learning throughout her lessons. She is always looking for ways to teach the ways of the Kingdom to her students and asking the Holy Spirit for new ways to do so. She is also aware that her students are watching the way she lives her life, inside the classroom and out.

The thought of teaching at every moment can feel overwhelming if you think the goal is perfection. When the goal is not perfection but rather living authentically in connection with God so that the world can see who He is, this becomes a great privilege. We are continually growing to become more like Him so that we can show the world around us how good He is. Everything that comes our way then becomes a platform to show who He is and to teach His ways.

The thought of teaching at every moment can feel overwhelming if you think the goal is perfection.

I remember when I began to realize this in my own household. I have four strong-willed children, closely spaced in age. Each of them has a strong opinion on almost everything and none of them, at least at home, is scared to share it. As you can imagine, this leads to multiple opportunities for disagreements pretty much every day. This was exhausting for me as a mother, particularly when they were small. I would cringe every time another argument broke out because I would need to intervene and help bring it to a resolution, again. It seemed like it was never-ending, and I was getting tired and cranky. I just wanted peace to reign in my house, and these kids refused to live in harmony with one another.

One day I realized that what I saw as an interruption to my day was, in fact, the most important part of my day. Every fight that broke out was another opportunity to train the world changers that lived in my house how to honor one another. My change in perspective allowed me to see my day differently. I went from teaching them to do the right thing in order to gain peace to stepping into my role as a Kingdom educator and intentionally training my children through every interaction. I am now much more conscious of the role that I have both with my children and others around me. I do my best to not only teach them how to deal with stress but also to model that for them. I know that when I have a disagreement with my husband or am struggling with a difficult person that I am training them in how to respond to their own circumstances.

So what does this mean in the classroom? You too have the opportunity to teach things that go well beyond the scope of the curriculum. Some of this teaching will simply be as a result of your students' watching how you "do life." When pressure is on, do you suddenly become nasty to be around? When you are tired, do you give less than your best? Your students are watching and learning what is acceptable behavior from watching you. Likewise, they see you when you go the extra mile for the student who was rude to you and didn't really seem to deserve your time. They watch when you are kind and gentle with the student with learning disabilities. They see when you pause and control yourself when you want to get angry. Every fight or argument that breaks out is an opportunity to teach about honor in relationships. Failures become opportunities to teach students about their worth beyond the test score. This kind of teaching requires more of you, and you may not see the actual results of your life in this world, but you never know what effect this is having on your students. The Bible tells us to be salt and light (Matthew 5:13–16). It says that when your light shines, those around you will praise your Father in heaven. Your living the Kingdom in your classroom does bring your Father praise.

The other side of this same coin is that you get to teach Kingdom inside of your curriculum. Every subject has the ability to be infused with God and His values. As Tawny showed above, even a simple spelling test becomes an opportunity to speak things to your students that reinforce a Kingdom culture in your classroom. Use the sentences that you call out to speak truth. If you aren't good at thinking of ways to do that on the fly, then think through the sentences you can use before the test.

Here are some examples I came up with using some of my son's spelling words for this week:

Codger: I thought the man next door was just an old codger until I got to know him.

Unanimous: The decision was not unanimous, but we chose to get along anyway.

Vanquish: It is time to vanquish any thought that you are a failure at math.

While on their own each is just a simple sentence, when you use these kinds of statements each time you teach spelling, you are adding to the culture of your classroom. You are letting your students know that this classroom is a place where relationships are valued and where we believe good things about ourselves. This is even more effective if the statements are reinforcing ideas you have already discussed as a class.

Math and science give opportunities for discussions on the beauty and patterns of nature. Let your passion for the things He has created shine through and ask lots of questions that get your students thinking outside of the box. You have the opportunity to connect with the minds of students and help them to explore the world around them.

Reading and writing provide great opportunities for teaching Kingdom principles for your students' success. Read books that highlight Kingdom qualities and initiate class discussions around those themes. If you can't choose your own textbooks then look for passages within the required reading that give opportunity for healthy discussions. Give writing assignments on topics that get students thinking. Talk about such themes as honor and how it does and doesn't show up in the characters of the book. Ask them what honor is and how it feels to be honored. Use the discussion to talk about what sort of culture they want to have in their class. Use other writing assignments or research assignments to have students think about their future in a positive way. What are their dreams? What do they need to do to get there? Who has achieved that dream that overcame horrible odds?

Every subject can become a vehicle to teach the truth.

Every subject can become a vehicle to teach the truth. The Holy Spirit is incredibly creative and is just waiting to help you as you teach the Kingdom through your curriculum and beyond.

QUESTIONS FOR ACTION

- What restrictions have you placed on yourself in regard to what you can teach in your classroom?

- Where do you feel "boxed in" regarding what you can teach? Are these restrictions real or perceived? How can you honor the real restrictions but teach what God is asking you to?

- What new perspective is God inviting you into as you consider what to teach beyond the curriculum?

- What is one subject this week wherein you will teach a Kingdom value/principle as part of your curriculum? What does God want to teach your students through that curriculum? What will you teach? How will you teach it?

- What have you been teaching your students when you are not teaching a lesson? I.e., what lessons are they learning through observing your life?

ACKNOWLEDGEMENTS

Thank you Debbie Gallasch, the world's best intern. You have been a constant source of encouragement, insight and wisdom along the way. Thanks for your help with the chapter endings and for being a sounding board for numerous other details. You are a delight to work with and we will miss you greatly.

Thank you Josh Stannard for sowing so mightily into this book by creating the cover graphics. We enjoyed getting to work with you on this project. You are a rock star!

Thank you Don Mayer and Debi Armstrong and Bethel Christian School for supporting us as we have developed and refined these tools to export throughout the world.

Thank you Andy Mason for all your help on technical details and providing up-grades, edits and other insights. We appreciate you.

Thank you Mason kids, Hannah, Emily, Ben and Holly for being patient with me as I worked on this book and for letting me share your stories. You are truly the best kids in the world.

ABOUT THE AUTHORS

Janine Mason is the director of Kingdom in the Classroom and the catalyst behind this book. She's passionate about getting teachers to understand that God is for them, has solutions for every area of need, and is eager to release His strategies and peace to their classroom. Janine has a close relationship with Bethel Christian School, where she serves on the board. Her role in Kingdom in the Classroom has led her to run conferences and local educators' gatherings as well as teach in Bethel's School of Supernatural Ministry. Along with her husband, Andy, she directs Dream Culture, a ministry that encourages and empowers people to discover their dreams and make practical steps to live out their purpose. She is co-author of a book of the same name. In addition, Janine is a mother to four amazing children. Her favorite things include watching her kids laugh, eating fresh summer fruit, completing DIY projects, and beating her husband at board games. For more on Janine, see www.iDreamCulture.com.

Tawny Novosad is a teacher at Bethel Christian School (BCS) and is full of life, love, and creativity. She has her master's in education and has a heart to help students search out and connect with their God-given identity. Originally from Texas, Tawny worked in public schools until she moved to Redding, California, in 2012. BCS was blessed and honored when she joined their staff, bringing vibrancy and energy while instilling in the students a love of learning, themselves, others, and God. Beyond school she enjoys anything outdoors—especially by the water—and spending quality time and laughing with her daughter Kya and other family and friends. She also gives grandmas a run for their money with her crochet skills!

Lindsay Brown joined the Bethel Christian School staff in 2011 and is currently teaching kindergarten. Lindsay is passionate about igniting and activating students in lifelong encounters and pursuit of God. She graduated from Gordon College in Massachusetts with a bachelor of science in elementary education, English, and special education and also completed Bethel's School of Supernatural Ministry prior to starting at BCS. With a background as a special education teacher and coordinator in the fishing town of Gloucester, Lindsay brings an array of unique skills and tools and a countenance that is full of "sonshine." In Lindsay's spare time, she likes to read, connect with friends, call family on the East Coast, and enjoy the beautiful Redding sunshine.

Sara Rust sees teaching as an adventure of finding gold in students and helping them to see the wonder of who they are as they grow and learn. She is passionate about empowering students to know their identity and walk it out (Psalm 145:47). Sara believes in partnering with the Holy Spirit to provide an education that is student centered, innovative, and excellent. Having lived overseas for ten years and then graduated with a bachelor of science degree in film (Northwestern University, 2003) and a master of education from Simpson University, Sara exudes creativity and versatility in a wide range of areas. She is gifted in music and singing and enjoys running, coffee shops, and writing in her spare time.

RECOMMENDED RESOURCES

DREAM CULTURE
By Andy & Janine Mason

This book will help you connect with Father God, unlock the dreams and desires of your heart and empower you to make them a reality. Each chapter contains simple and relevant teaching, inspirational, real-life stories and practical Dream Activation Exercises. The Dream Activation Exercises at the end of each chapter will show you how to turn your ideas into action steps and help you develop an intentional lifestyle of bringing your dreams to life.

GOD WITH YOU AT WORK
By Andy Mason

Be validated in your calling as a believer in your workplace. It will launch you into a whole new realm of experiencing more from a partnership with God in your daily activity. Andy's personal journey and the stories from other real-life business people will shatter your 'normal' and become your stepping stone to access greater things. The tangible Presence of God is the distinguishing factor that causes you to stand out. It's not compulsory, but it is an invitation. Do you want it?

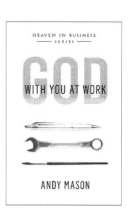

LET'S JUST LAUGH AT THAT FOR KIDS
By Steve Backlund

This is a powerful resource for adults who want the best for the young people in their lives. This book includes engaging stories, practical steps, and "laughter weapons" to teach children how to recognize and beat the lies the enemy tries to tell them. This is an interactive journey for adults and children to learn to "take every thought captive," to reinforce truth and hope in their lives. All the lie-defeating weapons of this book are laughter activated because we believe laughing at what the enemy is saying and planning helps us overcome the power of lies (Psalm 2:4).

KEEP YOUR LOVE ON
By Danny Silk

Keep Your Love On. It's a hard thing to do. Sometimes it's the hardest thing to do. But if you want to build healthy relationships with God and others, learning to keep your love on is non-negotiable. Adults and children, alike, thrive in healthy relationships in which it is safe to love and be loved, to know and be known. Yet for many, relationships are anything but safe, loving or intimate. They are defined by anxiety, manipulation, control and conflict. The reason is that most people have never been trained to be powerful enough to keep their love on in the face of mistakes, pain and fear.

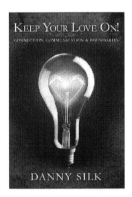

CULTURE OF HONOR
By Danny Silk

An environment that sustains life, hope, honor and destiny! In this powerful, revelation-packed book, Danny Silk describes the significant paradigm shift in church life, government, and relationships that has created and sustained the revival culture at Bethel Church in Redding, CA. Through many relevant and true-life stories, the church is revealed as a place of freedom, respect, empowerment, and healthy discipline (not punishment). Culture of Honor challenges the status quo of church leadership structure and presents a refreshing view of the five-fold ministry.

LOVING OUR KIDS ON PURPOSE
By Danny Silk

Here is a fresh look at the age-old role of parenting. Loving Our Kids on Purpose brings the principles of the Kingdom of God and revival into our strategy as parents. 2 Corinthians 3:17 tells us that "Where the Spirit of the Lord is there is freedom." Most parenting approaches train children to learn to accept being controlled by well meaning parents and adults. Unfortunately, God is not going to control us as we gain independence from our parents. We must learn to control ourselves. This book will teach parents to train their children to manage their freedoms and protect their important heart to heart relationships.

Made in the USA
San Bernardino, CA
24 January 2018